The Problem of Stagflation

Reflections on the Microfoundation of Macroeconomic Theory and Policy

Gottfried Haberler

American Enterprise Institute for Public Policy Research
Washington, D.C.

Gottfried Haberler is Galen L. Stone Professor of International Trade Emeritus at Harvard University and a resident scholar at the American Enterprise Institute.

331.13
H114p

Library of Congress Cataloging-in-Publication Data

Haberler, Gottfried, 1900–
  The problem of stagflation.

  (AEI studies ; 422)
  1. Unemployment—Effect of inflation on.
I. Title. II. Series.
HD5710.H33 1985   331.13'72   85–9142
ISBN 0-8447-3578-7 (alk. paper)

1 3 5 7 9 10 8 6 4 2

AEI Studies 422

Printed in the United States of America

Contents

Foreword

In the 1970s a new term was coined in economics—stagflation. It was used to describe a relatively new phenomenon in the industrial economies, declining economic activity accompanied by rising prices. Most previous recessions had been associated with declining prices.

This phenomenon led to a number of competing explanations of its root causes and, more important, posed a dilemma for policy makers, who could no longer use standard macroeconomic policies to reduce unemployment without the risk of accelerating inflation. It became clear then that past economic policy prescriptions did not apply and that new methods for dealing with stagflation were required.

In this study Professor Gottfried Haberler, one of our leading economic scholars, discusses and analyzes what the main paradigms of macroeconomic policy—monetarism, Keynesianism, and the school of rational expectations—have to say about the baffling problem of stagflation.

In his wide-ranging study Professor Haberler discusses the striking contrast between the vigorous recovery of the U.S. economy and the sluggishness of European economies. This contrast is largely due to great structural advantages of the United States over Europe, such as a huge internal free trade area and, equally important, the fact that transportation, communications, and electric power are in the hands of efficient, competitive private enterprise. In Europe the Common Market has fallen far short of achieving its goal of creating a free trade area, and transportation, communications, and electric power are reserved for national, public enterprises that, whatever their technological prowess, are impervious to competition and incapable of efficient operation across national borders.

Among Professor Haberler's important policy conclusions is that monetary and fiscal restraint should be assisted by micromeasures designed to bring the economy closer to the competitive ideal so as to minimize the pains of disinflation and adjustment. In Europe this type of policy is called supply-oriented policy, which is a much broader concept than supply-side economics as used in the United

States. He argues that supply-oriented and demand-oriented policies should be regarded not as alternatives but as complements. Other topics addressed are the strong dollar and the huge U.S. trade and budget deficits. The last chapter critically examines the theory that the United States needs an "industrial policy," that it can no longer rely on private enterprises to initiate new methods of production and to develop new products to ensure sustained growth. The theory is rejected because its principal assumptions are not borne out by the facts.

We at AEI are fortunate to benefit from the breadth of knowledge and the historical perspective of Professor Haberler. He has written a number of studies on the major economic issues of our times, and this study adds to the list of insightful economic analyses.

This study was originally written for and will also be published by the Pacific Institute in a book edited by Thomas Willett entitled *Political Business Cycles and the Political Economy of Stagflation*.

WILLIAM J. BAROODY, JR.
President
American Enterprise Institute

Summary

This paper starts with the problems of stagflation, the vicious kind of inflation that developed in all industrial countries in the post–World War II period. While in the past spells of declining economic activity were accompanied with rare exceptions by falling prices—deflationary depressions—we now have inflationary recessions. Stagflation poses a dilemma for macroeconomic policy: If it tries to curb inflation by tight monetary-fiscal policy, it increases unemployment. If it tries to reduce unemployment by easy money, it accelerates inflation. This paper analyzes critically what the leading paradigms of macroeconomic policy, monetarism, rational expectations, and Keynesianism have to say about this baffling problem.

Since Keynes was undoubtedly the most influential economist of the century, Keynesianism receives special attention. A sharp distinction is made, however, between Keynesian economics and the economics of Keynes. The master himself changed his views frequently—on some important occasions so quickly that many of his followers could not keep pace.

The nature and causes of the Great Depression of the 1930s are discussed in some detail, because it was a world-shaking event and has been and still is widely misinterpreted. World trade slumped by about 50 percent in nominal terms (gold dollars) and 30 percent in real terms, the difference reflecting a sharp price decline, especially of primary products, which dealt a heavy blow to countries in the third world. From August 1929 to March 1933 industrial production in the United States declined 53 percent, real GNP 50 percent, and nominal GNP 33 percent; unemployment rose to 25 percent and even higher in Germany. The high unemployment helped Hitler to come to power and gave him an opportunity to strengthen his position by early economic successes.

The depression had a profound effect on economic thinking. The cause of economic liberalism—liberalism in the classical sense of free enterprise, free markets, and free trade—sank to its lowest point. The achievements of the two totalitarian regimes—Hitler's economic success and the apparent immunity of Communist Russia to the depres-

1

sion that engulfed the West—convinced many that central planning was superior to capitalism.

The Great Depression gave birth to the Keynesian revolution, and there was a confluence of Keynesianism and Marxism. Some of Keynes's most gifted followers became what Schumpeter called Marxo-Keynesians. Keynes himself turned away from his "early beliefs" in liberalism and free trade and had a spell of protectionism, nationalism, and interventionism. One of his great admirers, Lord Lionel Robbins, put it this way: "even Keynes succumbed to the then current insanity—the aberration of a noble mind."

Less than ten years later Keynes reverted to his early liberal beliefs, but many of his followers still toe the line of protectionism. In his last paper, which was published posthumously, Keynes castigated some of his erstwhile followers who had become his critics, calling their theories "modernist stuff gone silly and turned sour," and pleaded that "the classical medicine" of monetary discipline and liberal policies should be given a chance.

Actually, the monetarists were right: the Great Depression was due to horrendous but avoidable policy mistakes, not to a basic instability of capitalism as Keynes and Marx thought. Concretely, the depression of the 1930s would not have been so severe or lasted so long if the Federal Reserve had not, through acts of commission and omission, allowed the basic money supply to shrink by about 30 percent. One need not be an extreme monetarist to understand that such a contraction of the money supply would have catastrophic consequences. Thus Joseph A. Schumpeter, who was not a monetarist, said that the avoidable breakdown of the U.S. banking system in the 1930s and the implied contraction of the money supply "turned retreat into rout"; what would otherwise have been a recession, perhaps a relatively severe one, became a deep depression. He blamed the anticapitalistic policies of the New Deal for the slow recovery of the U.S. economy after the depression. Full employment was reached only after the outbreak of the war in Europe, when U.S. rearmament went into high gear.

A brief comparison of the New Deal policy and the policy of Nazi Germany is instructive. Roosevelt and Hitler came to power at the same time in early 1933. Both found the economy in deep depression and embarked on expansionary policies. In Nazi Germany money wage rates remained stable, but average real weekly and annual earnings rose sharply because unemployment declined rapidly and the workweek lengthened. The same striking improvement took place in Austria after the Nazi takeover in 1938. Prices remained stable. Thus Hitler was able to provide butter and guns at the same time. This greatly strengthened his hold on the German people.

After three or four years, when rearmament went into high gear, the picture changed. Price control and rationing made the stable prices more and more fictitious. Nonetheless, the overall judgment must be that Hitler's economic policy was very successful. It is no exaggeration to speak of an economic miracle. Fortunately, the second German economic miracle—the spectacular and sustained rise of the German economy from the ashes of the Hitler Reich that started in 1948—demonstrates that a democracy using liberal methods can do even better than a ruthless dictatorship.

I now turn to the policy of the New Deal. Against the advice of Keynes, it made the mistake of combining monetary-fiscal expansion with price- and wage-boosting measures. Thus the price level rose in the midst of still high unemployment—an early case of stagflation. In 1937 the Federal Reserve was forced to step on the monetary brake, which caused a brief but extremely vicious depression. In thirteen months, from May 1937 to June 1938, industrial production slumped 32.4 percent and real GNP 13.2 percent, and unemployment rose from 10 percent to 20 percent. Nazi Germany was able to skip this depression altogether.

I return to the Keynesian misinterpretation of the nature of the Great Depression. It had the most unfortunate effect of giving post-war policy an inflationary bias. Every dip in economic activity was interpreted as a signal that a new depression was in the offing, requiring expansionary countermeasures. Given this outlook, it was not surprising that leading Keynesians in the United States and Britain completely misjudged the prospects of orthodox policies. A striking example was the currency reform in Germany in 1948 and the simultaneous abolition by Ludwig Erhard of all wage and price controls inherited from the Nazi period. Keynesians warned that it would have disastrous consequences and that economic growth in the Soviet zone of Germany would surpass growth in the West. Actually, Erhard's dash for economic freedom was a tremendous success, a turning point toward a revival of liberalism. Forty years later Keynesian economists similarly misjudged the prospects of the liberal policies of Margaret Thatcher.

I must guard against a possible misunderstanding. From accepting the monetarist explanation that the depression would not have occurred if the Federal Reserve had prevented the collapse of the U.S. banking system and the contraction of the money supply and rejecting the Keynesian explanation, it does not follow that Keynes's recommendation in the 1930s of government deficit spending was wrong. On the contrary, once a deep depression with mass unemployment, falling prices, and deflationary expectations had been allowed to develop, it was much better to inject money directly into the

3

income-expenditure stream by deficit spending than to rely on monetary policy (open market operations) alone. The latter would eventually have turned the economy around, but in the meantime a large pool of liquidity would have been created that would cause inflationary pressure later on.

Keynes was, however, not the first or the only one to understand that. It was, for example, the recommendation of Chicago economists—Henry Simons, Jacob Viner, and others—and was accepted by some neoclassical economists in Britain, such as A. C. Pigou. But it is fair to say that without Keynes's powerful sponsorship, it would have taken much longer. Actually, the idea was greatly oversold, and Keynesians pushed it long after the conditions had changed. In other words, until recently Keynesians did not understand that in the postwar period we no longer live in a Keynesian world.

I return to the Keynesian misinterpretation of the Great Depression. It had the unfortunate consequence that it was picked up in the third world. Raúl Prebisch, probably the most influential proponent of the new development economics, speaks of the two "great crises of capitalism" that changed his early liberal convictions. The first was the Great Depression; a crisis it surely was, but a crisis of government policy, not of capitalism. The second great crisis was the world recession of the late 1970s and early 1980s. To call this a great crisis of capitalism is ludicrous. There has, in fact, been no depression in the postwar world, if by depression we mean a decline in economic activity remotely resembling the Great Depression of the 1930s or earlier ones. The reason is that there has been no deflation, no sharp decline in the money supply, as in the 1930s. This confirms the monetary explanation of the Great Depression.

Some will ask, Have we not exchanged the horrors of deflation for those of inflation? Inflation is rampant in many parts of the world. It does much harm, but it would be a great exaggeration to say that it has done nearly as much damage as deflation did in the 1930s, even in the most inflationary countries.

Keynesians have until recently been unconcerned about inflation and have ignored the disturbing phenomenon of inflationary expectations. That was not true, however, of the master. In fact, Keynes was concerned about inflation all his life, except in the early 1930s when he wrote the *General Theory*, which became the gospel of the Keynesians. But already in 1937, one year after the publication of the *General Theory*, he had changed course and said it was time to switch policy from combating unemployment to curbing inflation.

Monetarists and rational expectations theorists can be criticized for playing down the role of wage and price rigidity and the power of

4

labor unions and other pressure groups. Attempts by some monetarists to demonstrate that even high unemployment and stagflation are compatible with the assumption of competitive, fast-clearing markets and that it is not necessary to fall back on union power, wage and price stickiness, and other institutional rigidities are quite unconvincing. This view stems from the failure to distinguish between voluntary and involuntary unemployment and leads to faulty policy conclusions.

Monetarists are right, however, that monetary restraint is a necessary condition for winding down inflation. In a sense it is even a sufficient condition—in the sense that whatever power unions have and whatever the size of the budget deficit, sufficiently tight money will bring down inflation. But the cost of disinflation in prolonged unemployment, lost output, and slow growth will be very high unless something is done about the rigidities and budget deficits.

That brings me to the problem of incomes policy. When Keynesians at long last became aware of the dangers of inflation, they began recommending incomes policy. This is, unfortunately, a vague term. It is often used in the sense of more or less comprehensive wage and price controls. In that sense it must be rejected. Wage and price controls deal only with symptoms and have never worked. But incomes policy can be defined differently, as a bundle of measures to curb the monopoly power exerted by labor unions and other groups through deregulation of industry, free trade, and so on—policies designed to bring the economy closer to the competitive ideal and thus reduce the pains of inflation and adjustment. In Europe this type of policy is often called supply-oriented policy, because it increases supply.

Supply-oriented policy, sometimes also called adjustment policy, must be distinguished from supply-side economics as used in the United States. The latter, to my mind, is a dangerously oversimplified theory. True, high marginal tax rates tend to reduce savings and work effort, and a reduction of marginal tax rates will be a part of any supply-oriented policy, along with many other measures. But to assume, as the supply-siders do, that a reduction of taxes by itself will offset the loss in revenue and not increase the budget deficit and will ensure rapid growth is totally unrealistic.

A supply-oriented policy should not be regarded as an alternative to demand-oriented policy, to demand management by monetary and fiscal measures. Demand-oriented and supply-oriented policies are complements, not substitutes. In chapters 12 and 14 these problems are discussed in considerable detail.

The striking contrast in recent years between the booming U.S.

economy and the sluggishness of the recovery in most European countries is briefly discussed. It has contributed to the strength of the dollar by attracting capital from abroad and to the large U.S. trade deficits.

The reasons for this disparity are some basic structural advantages of the United States and handicaps of Europe. These structural differences are of three kinds. First, most European economies are plagued, much more than the U.S. economy, by what one may call excesses of the welfare state, by very high taxes, and by a most oppressive regulatory climate. This has made the European economies very inflexible. An extreme example is the Netherlands. Unemployment is almost 18 percent, but unemployment and other welfare benefits are so generous that many jobless people have little incentive to work. In other words, a large part of the unemployment should be classified as "voluntary."[1] At the other extreme is Switzerland with an unemployment rate of about 1 percent. To guard against a possible misinterpretation, I add that the large number of foreign workers provides a buffer and helps to keep unemployment low; but it explains only a small fraction of the Swiss success.

The second advantage of the United States is that it enjoys an internal free trade area of continental size. The European Common Market was supposed to create a similar free trade area for Europe but has fallen far short of achieving its goal. The third great advantage of the U.S. economy is that important industries such as railroads, airlines, telephone and telegraph, and electric power are in private hands while in Europe they are public monopolies. Deregulation of the airlines, trucking, and railroads has provided efficient, competitive transportation services for the U.S. economy, in sharp contrast with Europe, where state enterprises are impervious to international competition.

The question is sometimes asked why only six years ago, despite structural advantages, the dollar was so weak that a dollar rescue operation had to be organized. The answer is that under the Carter administration the inflation rate in the United States again soared into the two-digit range. Whatever the structural advantages, inflation will nullify their effect on the exchange rate.

The policy implications of the analysis are straightforward. Monetary restraint is still necessary despite the fact that the current cyclical expansion has produced surprisingly little inflationary pressure. Inflation is down but not out. It may well accelerate again when the strong dollar weakens, as most experts expect.[2] Monetary restraint should be assisted by prudent fiscal policy and by microeconomic measures (supply-oriented policy) to bring the economy closer to the competitive ideal. It is argued that from the economic point of view business (industrial) monopolies, oligopolies, and cartels do not present difficult problems in the present-day world, because outside the area of public utilities hardly any monopoly could survive under free trade. Free trade is the most effective and administratively the simplest antimonopoly policy.

Monopoly power wielded by labor unions is a much more difficult problem. It is true that in the current cyclical expansion in the United States wage pressure has not been so strong as in earlier cases. The power of unions has decreased, and wage costs have not increased as much as in earlier cyclical expansions. But the picture is not uniformly bright. Unions in such industries as steel and automobiles have managed to keep wages about 50 percent above the average wage in U.S. manufacturing industries.

This has been possible because these industries have been protected from foreign competition. In its infinite wisdom the government has used what is the worst possible method of import protection, namely, the so-called voluntary export restrictions imposed on foreign exporters. It is the worst method because under this system the difference between the price inside and outside the protected areas goes to the foreign exporters, rather than to the U.S. Treasury, as it would under an import tariff. It has been estimated, for example, that the policy of voluntary export restriction gives Japanese automobile firms an annual subsidy of over $2 billion at the expense of American consumers.

The general lesson of this story is that free trade not only is the best antimonopoly policy but also reduces the power of labor unions. Similarly, the deregulation of the airline and trucking industries, which is equivalent to the establishment of internal free trade, has sharply curtailed the power of the unions of the teamsters and air pilots. Some specific measures are discussed that would make labor markets more efficient and competitive.

The final chapter presents a critical analysis of the theory that the United States needs an industrial policy, that it can no longer rely on private enterprise to introduce new products and new methods of production to ensure rapid growth. This theory has become popular in response to the last recession and to the slowdown of productivity growth. Thus it is reminiscent of the theory of secular stagnation that flourished in the 1930s. It is no longer possible to say, as the stagnationists of the 1930s did, that there is a lack of investment opportunities due to a slowdown of technological progress. There has been a veritable explosion of scientific and technological advance since World War II. What the proponents of industrial policy now say is

7

that there is a lack of entrepreneurial vigor and that the United States is falling behind other countries. Actually, there are many striking examples of lively entrepreneurial activity, such as the economic rejuvenation of New England (the replacement of the obsolescent shoe and textile industries by high-technology industries) and the emergence of Silicon Valley in Southern California—both entirely the work of private enterprise.

A variety of measures have been mentioned as coming under the umbrella of industrial policy, but the core of the policy is that some special government agency, a "development bank," should be set up to identify industries with a "high growth potential" and should help them along with tax breaks, cheap loans, research grants, subsidies, and import restrictions if necessary. Thus industrial policy can also be regarded as a new version of the infant industry argument. In fact, Alexander Hamilton is mentioned as an early proponent of industrial policy. But although the classical proponents recommended protection for industrial infants, the modern version applies it to the most developed country—senile industry protection would be a better term.

At any rate, it is naive to assume that a government agency would do a better job of developing new industries than private enterprise. The predictable result would be that the government would find itself holding a string of white elephants.

In fact the experiment has been made. The French government of François Mitterrand has adopted industrial policy in a grand manner, although they do not call it industrial policy but simply Socialism. A number of leading industrial corporations were nationalized because they were regarded as promising candidates to be turned into showpieces of rapid industrial development. They did not turn out that way. Despite huge infusions of additional capital at the taxpayers' expense, most of the nationalized enterprises have suffered large losses and have become a heavy burden on the government budget.

Notes

1. For details see *The Economist* (London), March 30, 1985, note on p. 62, "Dutch Welfare: Too Good to Last."

2. I have discussed this problem in my contribution, "International Issues Raised by Criticism of the U.S. Budget Deficits," to Phillip Cagan, ed., *Essays in Contemporary Economic Problems, 1985: The Economy in Deficit* (Washington, D.C.: American Enterprise Institute, 1985).

1
The Dilemma of Stagflation

The appearance for the first time on a large scale of stagflation—the coexistence of high inflation and high unemployment—has posed serious new problems for economists and policy makers.

The policy maker, who had just mastered the principles of modern "Keynesian" macroeconomics, was confronted with a nasty dilemma: if he applied expansionary measures to reduce unemployment, he would accelerate inflation; if he adopted restrictive measures to curb inflation, he would exacerbate unemployment. This dilemma did not exist, at least not in such an acute form, before World War II. In earlier business cycles prices declined in recessions and depressions. Therefore, expansionary measures, either of an automatic kind (letting the automatic stabilizers work) or of a discretionary kind (if not overdone), would reduce unemployment without immediately threatening a rise in prices.

The difficulties posed by stagflation for economic theory stem from the fact that traditionally, explicitly or implicitly, the microfoundation of macrotheory has been that of a competitive markets system.[1] The assumption of perfect competition in the labor market is inconsistent with persistent unemployment and stagflation. In general abstract theory, unemployment can be defined as an excess of the supply of labor over the demand. There are more job seekers than jobs. (See chapter 5 for further discussion of the concept and distinction of different kinds of unemployment.) Elementary economic theory teaches that under competition excess supply will drive down the price until demand and supply come into equilibrium. Unemployed workers will compete for jobs, and the wage will decline in relation to prices until full employment is restored.

This paper is an updated version of a paper written in the winter of 1983–1984 for the Pacific Institute for Public Policy Research, 177 Post Street, San Francisco, California, as a contribution to a volume of essays, *Political Business Cycles and the Political Economy of Stagflation*, edited by Thomas D. Willett, to be published later. The author and the American Enterprise Institute express their thanks to the Pacific Institute for permission to bring out the paper as an AEI publication.

That this is an inadequate picture of reality has been realized for a long time. It has once more been dramatically demonstrated by the long period of stagflation, which in recent years has given rise to a flood of more or less sophisticated attempts to account for the apparent stickiness of wages and prices and to explain the stagflation riddle.

Notes

1. This is true also of Keynes's *General Theory of Employment, Interest, and Money* (1936). James Tobin recently said, "It is unfortunate that Keynes, in spite of the Chamberlin-Robinson revolution that was occurring in microeconomics at the same time he was making his macro revolution, chose to challenge orthodoxy on its own microeconomic ground of competitive markets" (James Tobin, "Okun on Macroeconomic Policy: A Final Comment," in James Tobin, ed., *Macroeconomics, Prices, and Quantities: Essays in Memory of Arthur M. Okun* [Washington, D.C.: Brookings Institution, 1983], p. 299). Actually Keynes's position is ambivalent. He often simply assumed rigid *money* wages and prices, an assumption that is inconsistent with perfect competition. At the same time he accepted the classical position that real wages are determined by the marginal productivity of labor. That Keynes, as a rule, assumed rigid wages is the central theme of John R. Hicks's contribution to "The Keynes Centenary," in *The Economist* (London), June 18, 1983. The truth is that he simply was neither much interested nor well versed in microeconomics.

2
Some Proposed Solutions
of the Dilemma

It will be useful to start by identifying two extreme attempts to solve the riddle. At one extreme monetarists and members of the rational expectations school usually stick to the assumption of perfect competition by demonstrating, to their own satisfaction, that even "massive" and "persistent" unemployment is after all quite compatible with perfect competition and "instantaneous clearing of all markets." (For certain qualifications of this statement, see below.)

At the other extreme is the Keynesian solution. That solution is to assume, with a minimum of theoretical underpinning, that real wages are in fact rigid because, even if money wages are allowed to decline, prices will fall *pari passu* so that real wages will remain unchanged.[1]

Between the monetarist–rational expectations extreme and the Keynesian extreme lies a large literature that tries to identify and evaluate deviations from the competitive ideal that account for the persistence of unemployment and stagflation. Among the factors mentioned are monopolies and oligopolies in commodity and labor markets, union power, government regulation, minimum wages, price supports, and so on.

The literature has become very large. I make no attempt to review it here. It seems safe to say, however, that a major contribution is the posthumously published book by Arthur M. Okun, *Prices and Quantities: A Macroeconomic Analysis*.[2]

Notes

1. This does not do full justice to Keynes. This is the theory he puts forward in the first part of the *General Theory of Employment, Interest, and Money* (1936) and restates again and again. But in chapter 19, "Changes in Money Wages," he concludes that full employment may eventually be restored if money wages are driven down by competition, because the real value of the money stock will increase, pushing down interest rates and

stimulating investment. In that case "we should, in effect, have monetary management by the trade unions rather than by the banking system" (p. 267). According to Keynes there are, however, two hitches. Investment may not increase when interest rates decline, because of a secular dearth of investment opportunities. This theory, which became very popular in the 1930s among Keynesians, has been totally discredited by later developments. The other hitch is the "liquidity trap." There may be a floor below which interest rates cannot fall. This theory, too, is invalid, because it leads to the absurd conclusion that ever-increasing idle balances will pile up without inducing anybody to increase expenditures either on consumption or on investment. The theory of the "Pigou effect" or, more generally, the "wealth effect" has disposed of the Keynesian dilemma.

I should perhaps add that this whole discussion was purely theoretical; for nobody has proposed that the mass unemployment of the 1930s, which induced Keynes to write *The General Theory*, should be attacked "by manipulating the wage level rather than by manipulating [stimulating] effective demand," to use the words of A. C. Pigou (see his *Lapses from Full Employment* [London: Macmillan, 1945], p. 4). See also Gottfried Haberler, "The Pigou Effect Once More," *Journal of Political Economy* (June 1952), reprinted in Gottfried Haberler, *Prosperity and Depression*, 4th ed. (Cambridge, Mass.: Harvard University Press, 1958); and idem, "Price Inflexibility, Wage Rigidity and Unemployment," in *Prosperity and Depression*, 3d ed. (Geneva: League of Nations, 1941), pt. 3, pp. 491–502.

2. Arthur M. Okun, *Prices and Quantities: A Macroeconomic Analysis* (Washington, D.C.: Brookings Institution, 1981). See also the Okun memorial volume cited in note 1, chap. 1.

3
The Monetarist Position

First, let me make it quite clear that I fully agree with the monetarists that inflation, including stagflation, is basically a monetary phenomenon, in the sense that there has never been a significant inflation or stagflation—prices rising, say, by 4 percent or more a year for two or more years—without a significant growth in the stock of money. This is an empirical proposition. Exceptions are thinkable. For example, if as a consequence of war or revolution or a series of disasters output declined sharply, prices would rise sharply even with a constant quantity of money. But I cannot think of cases where that has happened in modern times. True, wartime inflations have been aggravated by a drop in output, but the great bulk of the price rise in wartime has always been caused by an increase in the money supply to finance government deficits.

The velocity of circulation of money is, of course, subject to change. Apart from extreme circumstances, however, such as hyperinflation or wartime price control and rationing, the changes in velocity are not large enough to invalidate the basic proposition of the quantity theory as stated above.[1]

In an important paper, "Information Costs, Pricing, and Resource Unemployment," Armen Alchian argued that even "in open, unrestricted competitive markets with rational, utility maximizing individual behavior," substantial or, in case of a sharp decline in monetary demand (depression), "massive" unemployment is possible.[2] To explain unemployment it is not necessary to fall back on "administered prices, monopolies, minimum wage laws, union restrictions and 'natural' inflexibility of wages and prices."[3] The basic idea is that information about job opportunities is not a free good. The information cost is not negligible. A worker who has lost his job may well spend much time and money searching for an acceptable job opening.

Concepts in the social sciences are always a little fuzzy on the edges and should be taken *cum grano salis*. Thus full employment does not mean that everybody who is able to work has a job—not even all those who are also willing to work at the ruling wage and working conditions for the type of work for which they are qualified. Or, to take another example, competitive markets that equate demand and supply are not incompatible with the coexistence of job vacancies (or vacant apartments for that matter) and unemployed job seekers (or people looking for an apartment).

It is certainly very useful to have all that spelled out in precise language, and Alchian has done an excellent job. But it is really not new and should not be controversial. After all, it is generally realized that frictional—and some structural—unemployment is compatible with "full employment."[4]

Notes

1. In the well-documented German case of hyperinflation of 1922–1923, velocity rose to fantastic heights. As a consequence the real value of the stock of money declined to a small fraction of its normal value. But since this was the consequence of printing money, it does not contradict the quantity theory as stated above. Actually the lag of the rate of change of the money supply behind that of change of the price level (as well as that of the value of the dollar in the foreign exchange market) was widely regarded, especially in Germany, as a striking contradiction of the classical quantity theory. (For details see my *Theory of International Trade* [London and New York, 1935], p. 59.)

2. Armen A. Alchian, "Information Costs, Pricing and Resource Unemployment," *Western Economic Journal*, vol. 7, no. 2 (June 1969), p. 117; reprinted in *Microeconomic Foundation of Employment and Inflation Theory* (New York: Norton, 1970), and in Armen A. Alchian, *Economic Forces at Work* (Indianapolis: Liberty Press, 1974).

3. Ibid., p. 109.

4. Alchian refers to two basic theoretical books on the subject: J. R. Hicks, *The Theory of Wages*, 1st ed. (London, 1932), 2d ed. (London, 1963); and W. H. Hutt, *The Theory of Idle Resources* (London, 1939). Keynes excludes "frictional" unemployment, workers "between jobs," from what he calls "involuntary" unemployment (see chap. 5 below).

4
An Early Case of Stagflation: The New Deal, 1933–1937

A question of crucial importance, which Alchian does not answer explicitly, is this: How large a part of observed unemployment is explained by his theory? He gives the reader the impression that a very large part can be explained without reference to union power, monopolies, government policies, minimum wages, and so on. The only concession he makes is that the "slow recovery" of the U.S. economy after the depression of 1929–1932, the prolonged unemployment, "appears inconsistent with the theory."[1] It was due to assorted wage- and price-boosting policies of the New Deal—the National Industrial Recovery Act (NIRA), the Agricultural Adjustment Act (AAA), the National Labor Relations Act. But the importance of these measures is played down by arguing that each of them had merely a once-for-all effect. "If all of these factors had occurred once and for all in, say, 1932, the subsequent recovery rate should have been more rapid. But they in fact did occur in sequence over several years."[2] This, according to Alchian, explains why the recovery was delayed until 1941. After six years of the New Deal the unemployment rate was still in the two-digit range, and it took the war boom to restore full employment—a dismal failure indeed.

I suggest that this argument greatly understates the total effect of the New Deal reforms. The immediate effect was to lead to an alarming price rise in the midst of high unemployment—an early case of stagflation, or cost-push inflation as it was called at that time. This induced the Federal Reserve to step on the monetary brake, which brought on the brief but very severe depression of 1937–1938.[3]

Even more important, the New Deal measures reduced for a long time to come, in part perhaps indefinitely, price and wage flexibility. This reduced flexibility was and is responsible for the fact that a decrease in aggregate spending (nominal GNP) finds expression to such a large extent in quantities—declining output and unemployment—rather than in declining inflation rates.

Let me quote Frank H. Knight who, like Henry Simons, Jacob Viner, and other members of the older generation of the Chicago school, did not ignore or minimize the great importance of the growing rigidity of wages and prices for the smooth working of the monetary system. Knight wrote:

> In a free market these differential changes [between prices of "consumption goods" and "capital goods" on the one hand and prices of "productive services, especially wages," on the other hand] would be temporary, but even then might be serious, and with important markets [especially the labor market] as unfree as they actually are, the results take on the proportion of a disaster.[4]

Knight wrote with the deflation of the 1930s in mind, but what he said about wage and price rigidity applies equally to disinflation and recession in the 1970s and 1980s.

I shall return to the Great Depression of the 1930s after reviewing another monetarist attempt to demonstrate that unemployment and stagflation are compatible with perfect competition. In a paper that has attracted much attention, Karl Brunner, Alex Cuikerman, and Allan H. Meltzer assert that "persistent unemployment" and stagflation "can occur in a neo-classical framework . . . in which expectations are rational and all markets clear instantaneously; in other words, under perfect competition."[5]

The relevant part of the authors' theory, the supply function of labor, is easy to understand without wading through the flood of equations with which they present their theory: Workers determine the amount of labor that they are willing to supply by comparing "the currently prevailing wage to the wage they currently perceive as permanent." If the prevailing wage is equal to the perceived permanent wage, there is full employment. Now suppose the economy is subjected to a "shock"—the authors usually speak of "a change in productivity." If productivity goes up, the actual real wage is raised "on impact." Still, the workers cannot know immediately whether the change is permanent or transient. Therefore, the currently perceived permanent wage will for some time be below the actual ruling wage. This will induce workers to supply more labor, "to work now and substitute future for current leisure," resulting in "negative unemployment."[6] In other words, there will be what is usually called "overfull employment."

If the shock is unfavorable—that is, if productivity declines—the actual real wage will be reduced "on impact." Again the workers cannot be sure what the permanent wage will be. Therefore, the

16

actual wage will for some time be below the currently perceived permanent wage. This will induce "part of the labor force which looks for work [to] abstain from accepting current employment. This group is counted as unemployed in the official statistics."[7] If "negative unemployment" means "substitution of future leisure for current leisure," then positive unemployment means substitution of current leisure for future leisure.

Notes

1. Armen A. Alchian, "Information Costs, Pricing, and Resource Unemployment," *Western Economic Journal*, vol. 7, no. 2 (June 1969), p. 126.

2. Ibid, p. 127.

3. Milton Friedman commented on the 1933–1937 episode of cost-push inflation as follows:

> The only example I know of in United States history when such a cost-push was important even temporarily for any substantial part of the economy was from 1933 to 1937, when the NIRA, AAA, Wagner Labor Act, and associated growth of union strength unquestionably led to increasing market power of both industry and labor and thereby produced upward pressure on a wide range of wages and prices. This cost-push did not account for the concomitant rapid growth in nominal income at the average rate of 14 percent a year from 1933 to 1937. That reflected rather a rise in the quantity of money at the rate of 11 percent a year. . . . The cost-push does explain why so large a part of the growth in nominal income was absorbed by prices. Despite unprecedented levels of unemployed resources, wholesale prices rose nearly 50 percent from 1933 to 1937, and the cost of living rose by 13 percent. Similarly, the wage cost-push helps to explain why unemployment was still so high in 1937, when monetary restriction was followed by another severe contraction.

See Milton Friedman, "What Price Guideposts?" in George P. Shultz and Robert Z. Aliber, eds., *Guidelines, Informal Controls, and the Market Place: Policy Choices in a Full Employment Economy* (Chicago: University of Chicago Press, 1966), p. 22.

4. Frank H. Knight, "The Business Cycle, Interest and Money," *Review of Economic Statistics*, vol. 23 (May 1941). Reprinted in Frank H. Knight, *On the History and Methods of Economics* (Chicago: University of Chicago Press, 1956), p. 224. See also p. 211: "Wages are notoriously sticky, especially with respect to any downward change of the hourly wage rates."

5. Karl Brunner, Alex Cuikerman, and Allan H. Meltzer, "Stagflation, Persistent Unemployment, and the Permanence of Economic Shocks," *Journal of Monetary Economics*, vol. 6, no. 4 (October 1980), pp. 467–92.

6. Ibid., p. 470.

7. Ibid.

5
Voluntary versus Involuntary Unemployment

To describe unemployment as leisure is rather odd. At any rate, it is voluntary unemployment: if workers "substitute current leisure for future leisure," the leisure that they freely choose, because they expect the future wage to be higher than the current one, constitutes *voluntary* unemployment and has nothing to do with real, *involuntary* unemployment. But the authors do not mention the indispensable distinction between voluntary and involuntary unemployment. That the words come from Keynes's *General Theory* has probably made the distinction suspect.

Keynes criticized the "classical" economists for recognizing only "voluntary" unemployment. There he was quite wrong, but he was prophetically right about some present-day monetarists. Actually, the distinction has been made, though often in other words, in serious discussions of the unemployment problem, both theoretical and empirical. In fact, the archclassical A. C. Pigou, who was one of the main targets of Keynes's criticism, used the very words "involuntary idleness" in a popular book[1] on unemployment in 1914 and had an excellent discussion of the distinction in his monograph *The Theory of Unemployment*.[2] D. H. Robertson, another classical economist, used the words "involuntary unemployment" in his *Study of Industrial Fluctuations*.[3] No wonder that Richard Kahn, Keynes's devoted disciple and assistant, "suffered a shock" when he discovered that what was regarded as one of the master's important discoveries was all in the classical writings that he had criticized.[4]

Compilers of unemployment figures have to struggle to prevent voluntary unemployment from contaminating their statistics, no doubt rarely with complete success. The published unemployment figures surely contain a significant amount of spurious, voluntary employment; generous unemployment benefits and welfare payments have made this an increasingly serious problem.

Let me elaborate a little, for the wage problem is of paramount importance. Brunner, Cuikerman, and Meltzer say in a footnote, as a sort of afterthought, that they are concerned with "cyclical" unemployment only. They do not say whether they regard the mass unemployment of the 1930s as cyclical. If the answer is yes, it contradicts their theory, because it makes no sense to assert that the unemployed at that time simply "substituted present for future leisure." If the answer is no, it makes the theory irrelevant because it fails to come to grips with the crucially important episode that gave rise to the modern discussion of unemployment.

Now consider the case of the U.S. steel and automobile industries. Wages in those industries are more than 50 percent higher than the U.S. average, and unemployment is very high. The authors will probably say that this is not cyclical but structural unemployment. At any rate it would not make sense to say that the unemployed steel or automobile worker, because of "a forecasting error," chose leisure. One could perhaps say that the unemployment is voluntary from the standpoint of the *union*, that the union leaders are willing to pay the price of high unemployment to keep wages high or possibly to maximize the wage bill. But for the unemployed steel and automobile workers the situation is quite different. They would surely be happy to work at the ruling wage or even a slightly lower one if jobs were available.[5]

In summary I find the tendency of modern monetarists to stick to the assumption of perfect competition and their attempts to explain away the importance of trade unions for the problem of unemployment and stagflation highly unrealistic. This has again been strikingly demonstrated by the recent coal strike in Britain and the metalworkers' strike in West Germany, which have sharply slowed the cyclical recovery in both countries.

Notes

1. A. C. Pigou, *Unemployment* (London: Howe University Library, 1914), p. 17.
2. A. C. Pigou, *The Theory of Unemployment* (London: Macmillan, 1933).
3. D.H. Robertson, *A Study of Industrial Fluctuations* (London, 1915), p. 210.
4. See Richard Kahn, "Unemployment as Seen by the Keynesians," in G. D. N. Worswick, ed., *The Concept and Measurement of Involuntary Unemployment* (London: Allen & Unwin, 1975), p. 20. Kahn's paper presents an excellent analysis of the concept of involuntary unemployment in Keynes's *General Theory* and of subsequent developments of Keynes's thinking (see below).
5. Further elaborations are possible. One could perhaps say that, as faithful members of their unions, workers are ready to accept the burdens of unemployment to uphold the decision of their union. Generous unemployment benefits make such a sacrifice easier.

6
The Concept of
Involuntary Unemployment
Further Considered

What I said above about the fuzziness of concepts in the social sciences applies with special force to that of involuntary unemployment. Keynes's definition is this: "Men are involuntarily unemployed if, in the event of a small rise in the price of wage-goods relative to the money wage, both the aggregate supply of labour willing to work for the current money wage and the aggregate demand for it at that wage would be greater than the existing volume of employment."[1] Elsewhere I have expressed the opinion that this definition is unnecessarily complicated; that the common-sense definition is quite satisfactory—to wit, that a man is involuntarily unemployed if he cannot find a job although he is willing and able to work at the ruling wage and work conditions for the type of work for which he is qualified.[2]

The Keynesian definition has, however, been defended by Alchian[3] and others on the ground that it makes the important distinction between a reduction of the real wage due to a rise in prices and a reduction due to a reduction in the money wage. Workers "as a rule" accept the former but resist that latter. The reason for this behavior is said to be that a rise in the price level affects all wage earners alike but reductions in money wages are never across the board and therefore alter relative wages. The consequence is that workers resist a reduction of their wages because nobody likes to be singled out for a wage cut.

There may be some truth in this argument. But the other half of the Keynesian theory is hard to accept. In our age of persistent inflation, widespread indexation, and sensitized inflationary expectations, it cannot be assumed that workers meekly and ignorantly accept a reduction in their real wage through inflation. Keynes himself was more cautious than Alchian. He speaks of a "small" rise in prices and says "as a rule" and "unless they [the reductions in real wages]

20

proceeded to an extreme degree."[4] If Keynes had lived longer, he would surely have amended his theory to take account of persistent inflation. As Axel Leijonhufvud has shown, we have to distinguish between Keynesian economics and the economics of Keynes.[5]

The fact is that Keynes was all his life concerned about inflation, except that when he wrote the *General Theory* in the 1930s he concentrated his fire on deflation. In 1937, however, one year after the publication of the *General Theory*, he wrote three articles in the *Times* in which he urged a change in policy to fight inflation, although unemployment was still high and inflation comparatively low by post-World War II standards.[6]

Notes

1. John M. Keynes, *The General Theory of Employment, Interest, and Money* (1936), p. 15.

2. See my paper, "The Economic Malaise of the 1980s: A Positive Program for a Benevolent and Enlightened Dictator," in William Fellner, project director, *Essays in Contemporary Economic Problems: Demand, Productivity, and Population* (Washington, D.C.: American Enterprise Institute, 1981). For the empirical application of these concepts, further specifications are required, and the borderline between voluntary and involuntary unemployment is not always clearly marked. On this point, see the careful analysis by Herbert Giersch, *Konjunktur- und Wachstumspolitik in der offenen Wirtschaft* (Wiesbaden: Dr. Th. Gabler-Verlag, 1977), pp. 254–57. I was glad that Richard Kahn, too, reached the conclusion that Keynes's definition was "unnecessarily complicated." He points out that elsewhere in the *General Theory* a simpler definition is used. (Richard Kahn, "Unemployment as Seen by the Keynesians," in G. D. N. Worswick, ed., *The Concept and Measurement of Involuntary Unemployment* [London: Allen & Unwin, 1975], p. 21.)

3. Armen A. Alchian, "Information Costs, Pricing, and Resource Unemployment," *Western Economic Journal*, vol. 7, no. 2 (June 1969), p. 122.

4. Keynes, *General Theory*, p. 14.

5. See Axeld Leijonhufvud, *On Keynesian Economics and the Economics of Keynes: A Study in Monetary Theory* (New York: Oxford University Press, 1968).

6. Keynes's three articles in the *Times* are reprinted in T. W. Hutchison, *Keynes versus the Keynesians? An Essay on the Thinking of J. M. Keynes and the Accuracy of Its Interpretation by His Followers* (London: Institute of Economic Affairs, 1977). For further details see T. W. Hutchison, *On Revolutions and Progress in Economic Knowledge* (Cambridge: Cambridge University Press, 1978), chap. 6, "Demythologizing the Keynesian Revolution," pp. 175–99. For Keynes's view on inflation, see Thomas M. Humphrey, "Keynes on Inflation," *Economic Review* (Federal Reserve Bank of Richmond), vol. 67, no. 1 (January/February 1981), pp. 3–13.

7
Rational Expectations

Before discussing further the growing rigidity of wages, I will discuss the modern theory of rational expectations and the contrasting Keynesian position. The theory of rational expectations is an offshoot of monetarism. The basic tenet of the school is that market participants—households and firms—must be assumed to act, by and large, rationally; they make use of all available information to form a judgment of future events, including the likely course of government macroeconomic policy and its effect on the economy. Specifically, market participants do not simply extrapolate the current price trend (inflation rate) but base their expectation of future inflation on an appraisal of a much broader kind.

Put in these terms, the theory is now widely accepted, even by Keynesians (see chapter 8), and may be regarded as self-evident. But this was not the case a few years ago. Let us not forget that what Harry Johnson called "the monetarist counterrevolution" and, we may add, its offshoot, the rational expectations theory, were a reaction to the Keynesian downgrading of money and unconcern about inflation.

From what I called the "basic tenet," rational expectations theorists have drawn radical, even astonishing, conclusions that are quite controversial, to put it mildly. What has been called the "hard-line" (unqualified) version of the theory[1] asserts flatly that macroeconomic policies—more precisely, systematic, that is to say predictable, macro-policies—have no effect on the real economy (output and employment) but affect only prices, money wages, and nominal interest rates. The argument is often described in the following way, taking as an example the case most favorable for the rational expectations theory: Suppose the government embarks on an expansionary monetary-fiscal policy to stimulate production and employment. The market participants will figure out exactly what the effects on the price level will be. Financial markets will react almost instantaneously, pushing up interest rates. Commodity markets will follow suit, with wholesale prices in the vanguard. Workers and their unions will press for higher wages. Higher interest and labor costs will inhibit an expansion of output. The conclusion of the hard-line rational expectations theory is that this will happen so fast that it can be said that macropolicies are ineffective, even in the short run, as far as the real economy is concerned. This sounds rather implausible.

The hard-line version of the theory has been softened considerably in later contributions. It is now often conceded that a policy change may be followed by a transition period because it takes some time for market participants to figure out what the authorities are up to.

Furthermore, the ineffectiveness applies only to "systematic," "predictable" policies. The theory does not deny that unsystematic, unpredictable policy changes have an effect on the real economy. The trouble with this argument, however, is that it is impossible to divide policies into two watertight compartments, wholly predictable and entirely unpredictable. It is a question of more or less predictable, not of either-or. Suppose the general thrust of a policy change—whether it is expansionary or contractionary—is not in doubt. Still, the vigor and persistence with which the policy will be pursued is always uncertain, and the assessments of different market participants will diverge. To assume, as the members of the school do, that the average or collective judgments will be exactly right, because errors made by individuals will cancel out, I find entirely unconvincing. The possibility of bandwagon effects and of cumulative and self-reversing errors of optimism and pessimism, which have played a great role in older business cycle theories, cannot be excluded.[2]

The most serious weakness of the hard-line version of the rational expectations theory—the ineffectiveness hypothesis—is that it pays no attention to wage and price rigidities. The theory is essentially one of perfect competition, of instantaneously clearing markets. This assumption, too, has been softened. It is now said that the theory can accommodate minor deviations from the competitive ideal.[3] Widespread rigidity of wages as we find it in the modern world (see chapter 9) is, however, an altogether different matter. Wage and price rigidity makes it impossible for monetary-fiscal policy, even if entirely systematic and correctly perceived by the public, to be neutral (ineffective) with respect to the real economy, as claimed by the rational expectations school.

Let me illustrate this by means of an extreme example: In the early 1930s, during the period of mass unemployment in the Great Depression, wages were rigid even in the upward direction. In other words, the supply of labor was highly, if not infinitely, elastic. Would anybody doubt that under such conditions an expansionary policy of deficit spending, as recommended by Keynes and many other economists at that time, would boost output and employment even if, or perhaps especially if, fully perceived by the public? The spending policy of the New Deal was indeed very effective in reviving the real economy. True, it also boosted prices, as we have seen. But this was due to the cost-raising policies of the New Deal and had little or nothing to do with the reactions described by the rational expectations theory.

The present situation is, of course, entirely different from that of the 1930s. Unemployment has been much lower in the postwar period than in the 1930s, and inflationary expectations have been sensitized by years of intermittent inflation. Even so, one cannot say that expansionary policies have been entirely ineffective in the postwar period as far as the real economy is concerned. Cyclical recoveries after recessions have been initiated or temporarily speeded up by expansionary policies. To say, as rational expectations theorists may be inclined to do, that these effects were due to the unsystematic parts of the expansionary policy does not help in view of the fact that systematic and unsystematic policy measures are in most cases not separable. At any rate, it takes time to figure out what the authorities are up to, and the learning process will not be the same for all market participants. Measures that look systematic and predictable to some market participants may appear unsystematic and surprising to others.

The most startling conclusion of the rational expectations school is the so-called Ricardian equivalence theorem, which states that it makes no difference whether the government finances its deficit by taxes or by borrowing. (It is called Ricardian because it has been attributed to David Ricardo. This is actually a misnomer. Ricardo formulated the theorem but then rejected it as unrealistic.) The theorem is based on the assumption that rational "agents"—firms and households—realize that government debts have to be serviced. Therefore, government borrowing will lead to higher taxes in the future. Increased future tax liabilities will induce rational people to save more, so that the increased supply of bonds resulting from government deficits and borrowing will be matched, dollar for dollar, by an increased demand for bonds. Hence deficits do not push up interest rates.

If the reader is surprised at how much knowledge people are supposed to have, he should know that this is not all. To counter the possible objection that the taxes to service the debt may fall on future generations of taxpayers, an "intergenerational" extension of the theory argues that the present taxpayer knows not only how much his or her future tax will be but also what the tax of his children and grandchildren will be and will save enough to protect them from extravagances of the present generation.

I can only repeat what I have said elsewhere: this is rational expectations gone wild. *Difficile est satiram non scribere.*[4]

Notes

1. See especially William Fellner, "The Valid Core of Rationality Hypotheses in the Theory of Expectations," *Journal of Money, Credit and Banking*, vol. 12, no. 4, pt. 2 (November 1980). That issue presents the proceedings of a full-dress review of the rational expectations theory at a seminar sponsored by the American Enterprise Institute, with contributions also by Bennet T. McCallum, Robert J. Barro, James Tobin, Edwin Burmeister, Arthur Okun, Phillip Cagan, and Gottfried Haberler. Another comprehensive review can be found in Stanley Fischer, ed., *Rational Expectations and Economic Policies* (Chicago: University of Chicago Press, 1980).

2. See especially A.C. Pigou, *Industrial Fluctuations*, 2d ed. (London: Macmillan, 1929). Pigou's theory of the business cycle is often described as pyschological. This is, however, inappropriate. Errors of optimism and pessimism are only one factor among others in Pigou's theory. He attributes equal weight, for example, to "monetary and banking policy."

3. See especially Bennet T. McCallum's contribution to the American Enterprise Institute seminar cited in note 1 and his papers, "Price-Level Stickiness and the Feasibility of Monetary Stabilization Policy with Rational Expectations," *Journal of Political Economy*, vol. 85, no. 3 (June 1977), pp. 627–34, and "Monetarism, Rational Expectations, Oligopolistic Pricing, and the MPS Econometric Model," *Journal of Political Economy*, vol. 87, no. 1 (February 1979), pp. 57–73.

4. "It is difficult not to write satire." The main references are Robert J. Barro, "Are Government Bonds Net Wealth?" *Journal of Political Economy*, vol. 82 (November/December 1974), pp. 1095–117, and Robert J. Barro, *Macroeconomics* (New York: John Wiley & Son, 1984), pp. 380–93. (For further details see Gottfried Haberler, "International Issues Raised by Criticisms of the U.S. Budget Deficits," in Phillip Cagan, ed., *Essays in Contemporary Economic Problems: The Economy in Deficit* [Washington, D.C.: American Enterprise Institute, 1985].)

8

The Evolution of
Keynesian Economics

I offer a brief description of the evolution of Keynesian economics, keeping in mind that it must be distinguished from the economics of Keynes himself. Keynesian economics has not stood still. I suggest that roughly three stages can be distinguished. The *first* stage accepts the picture of the economy that underlies Keynes's *General Theory*. It is depression economics in the strict sense. The *second* stage centers on the Phillips curve. It is still depression economics. It assumes constant or exogenously changing wages and prices, is unconcerned about inflation, and ignores inflationary expectations. The *third* stage can be described as Keynesian economics tinged with rational expectations ideas, coming to grips with inflationary expectations.

The First Stage. The *General Theory* was written during the Great Depression. It was depression economics. The picture underlying the *General Theory* is that of a mature capitalistic economy suffering from chronic oversaving and insufficient investment opportunities due to a secular slowdown of technological progress—an economy in constant need of resuscitation through government deficit spending.[1]

The theory of secular stagnation is a gross misinterpretation of the nature of the Great Depression of the 1930s. We know now that the depression would never have been so severe or lasted so long if the Federal Reserve had not by tragic policy mistakes of omission and commission caused or permitted the basic money supply to contract by about 30 percent.[2] One need not be an extreme monetarist to recognize that such a contraction of the money supply must have catastrophic consequences. Joseph A. Schumpeter, who certainly was not a monetarist but recognized monetary forces when he saw them, put it this way: The collapse of the U.S. banking system in the early 1930s and the implied contraction of money supply "turned retreat into rout"; what would have been a recession, perhaps a relatively severe one, became a catastrophic depression.[3]

Before going into further details about the evolution of Keynesian economics, I would like to point out that the misinterpretation of the Great Depression had, most unfortunately, a strong effect on the emerging development economics. The misinterpretation was eagerly embraced by many development economists, along with the *dirigiste* and protectionist wave in economic thinking, as exemplified by Keynes's temporary conversion from economic liberalism and free trade to planning and protection. Development economics thus acquired a *dirigiste*, protectionist slant from the beginning.

The prime example is the career of Raúl Prebisch, one of the most influential practitioners of development economics through his work in the United Nations, in the United Nations Conference on Trade and Development (UNCTAD) and the Economic Commission on Latin America (ECLA). In his brilliant contribution, "Five Stages in My Thinking on Development," to the World Bank's *Pioneers in Development* series, he relates that in the 1920s he "was a firm believer in neoclassical theories." But "the first great crisis of capitalism," the world depression of the 1930s, changed all that. The "second great crisis of capitalism, which we are suffering now, has strengthened my attitude."[4] What he referred to is the world recession that came to an end soon after the U.S. economy took off on an unexpectedly vigorous expansion, which is still in progress.

To call this a "second great crisis of capitalism" is a grotesque misinterpretation. For there was no depression, nothing remotely resembling the Great Depression or earlier ones. What happened was a comparatively mild recession, which came about when the United States and other industrial countries were forced to put on the monetary brakes to bring inflation under control.[5]

Some Keynesians, especially Lord Kaldor, have argued that if the Federal Reserve had prevented the contraction of the money supply by open-market operations, it would have made no difference, because the velocity of circulation of money would have declined.[6] To appraise the merits of this view, it is essential to distinguish sharply two problems. By failing to make this distinction, Kaldor vitiates his argument. The *first* problem is what would have happened if the Federal Reserve had prevented the contraction of the money supply by stopping the run on the banks and forestalling the collapse of the banking system.

The *second* problem is this: Suppose a recession has been allowed to degenerate into a deep depression characterized by declining prices, mass unemployment, and deflationary expectations, as happened in the early 1930s. Most economists, including many monetarists, agree that in such a situation it is better to inject money directly into the income stream by government deficit spending than to rely entirely on monetary policy (open-market operations). In the short run monetary policy would indeed be ineffective; if people expect prices to fall, even a zero nominal interest would not stimulate investment. True, after a long delay monetary policy would turn the economy around through the Pigou effect, but a large pool of liquidity would be created, which at a later stage would cause inflation.

From this it does not follow, however, that monetary policy would have been equally ineffective if it had prevented the collapse of the banking system and the contraction in the money supply. On the contrary, it would have forestalled the transformation of a recession into a deep depression. It was the preventable collapse of the banking system and the implied contraction in the money supply that "turned retreat into rout," to repeat Schumpeter's colorful phrase.

That the monetary factor, deflation, was the dominant cause of the depression is confirmed by the fact that in one country after another the depression was lifted as soon as deflation was stopped by orthodox or unorthodox measures—in the Scandivanian countries, Australia, and Nazi Germany—and that in the post–World War II period there were no major depressions, only comparatively mild recessions, despite much greater destruction than in World War I.

To support his theory of the ineffectiveness of monetary policy, Kaldor quotes what Milton Friedman had to say about Canada in his *Monetary History of the United States*: that "Canada had no bank failures because it had an efficient branch banking system (rather than the archaic U.S. unit banking system). Therefore, during the depression (1929–1933) in Canada the quantity of money declined by only 13 percent compared with 33 percent in the United States. On the other hand, velocity declined by 41 percent compared with 29 percent in the United States."[7] This proves, according to Kaldor,[8] that velocity adjusts automatically to changes in the quantity of money.

Actually, this does not prove Kaldor's point, for a reason that Kaldor overlooked—that the Canadian economy was rigidly linked to the U.S. economy by a fixed exchange rate and was therefore forced to share fully the depression in the United States. Net national product in Canada fell by 49 percent, compared with 53 percent in the United States. No wonder that pessimism (deflationary expectations) became entrenched as in the United States and velocity declined sharply. As Friedman points out, because there were no bank failures in Canada, the public's confidence in the banks was not shaken, and the demand for the bank-deposit portion of the money stock declined not nearly as much as in the United States; hence, velocity declined more sharply.[9]

Before discussing the second stage of Keynesian economics, I should point out that Keynes was not the first or the only economist to realize that in a deep depression government deficit spending is in order. That was the general view in Chicago, expressed by Frank H. Knight, Henry Simons, Jacob Viner, and others, which is the reason why Keynes did not make such an impression in Chicago as in other centers of learning.[10] Arthur Burns says in a recent paper, "I found myself recommending Keynesian policies in 1930 and 1931, well before *The General Theory* was published."[11]

In England A.C. Pigou, Dennis H. Robertson, and others reached the same conclusion. It did not require a "new economics" to understand that. But there can be no doubt that it was Keynes who made the idea popular in the professional literature as well as in the policies of most countries.[12]

The Second Stage. The Keynesian unconcern about inflation and neglect of inflationary expectations are highlighted by the theory of the Phillips curve, which postulates a more or less permanent trade-off between unemployment and inflation; lower unemployment can be obtained by accepting higher inflation. This theory for years dominated the Keynesian discussions of inflation. I cite two examples of prominent Keynesians. In 1960 Paul Samuelson and Robert Solow in a widely acclaimed article, "Analytical Aspects of Anti-Inflation Policy,"[13] presented a "modified Phillips curve for the United States," which they described as "the menu of choice[s] between different degrees of unemployment and price stability" (see figure 1). The authors mentioned specifically two "obtainable" choices: *A*, price stability with 5½ percent unemployment; and *B*, 3 percent unemployment with 4½ percent inflation per annum. They did not say whether they regard other points on their curve—for example, *C*, 1½ percent unemployment with 10 percent inflation—as "obtainable" choices.

As we see it now, point *C* would not be "obtainable." With 10 percent inflation, the short-run Phillips curve would not stay put. Inflationary expectations leading to anticipatory action by market participants would shift the curve up. But the authors, although they envisage shifts of the curve due to structural changes in the economy, do not point out that inflationary expectations would shift the curve.[14] It is true that there is a brief reference to inflationary expectations, but it comes earlier in the paper and is not related to the Phillips curve. The authors say that inflationary expectations would be caused by "a period of high demand and rising prices." Inflationary expectations would "bias the future in favor of further inflation." But they immediately play down the importance of the matter by saying, "Unlike

FIGURE 1
MODIFIED PHILLIPS CURVE FOR THE UNITED STATES

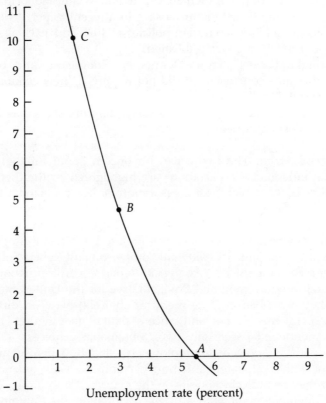

NOTE: This shows the menu of choices between different degrees of unemployment and price stability, as roughly estimated from the last twenty-five years of U.S. data.

SOURCE: Samuelson and Solow, ''Aspects of Anti-Inflation Policy,'' p. 192.

some other economists, we do not draw the firm conclusion that unless a firm stop is put, the rate of price increase must accelerate. We leave it as an open question: It may be that creeping inflation leads only to creeping inflation.''[15] This statement leaves out a crucial point. It has not been claimed that every creeping inflation inexorably becomes a trotting one; what is claimed is that inflation loses its stimulating power when it is stopped. In other words, the short-run Phillips curve does not stay put but shifts up.

It can be argued that this may not be true of very low inflation rates, say, not more than 2 or 3 percent, or even a little higher if they do not last too long. Maybe that is what the authors mean by "creeping." I think enough has been said to justify the conclusion that the paper by Samuelson and Solow illustrates my point that Keynesian economics is characterized by unconcern about the dangers of inflation and neglect of inflationary expectations.

Here is my second example. As late as 1972, shortly before inflation in the United States and other industrial countries soared into the two-digit range, James Tobin extolled the virtues of inflation in adjusting "blindly, impartially and non-politically the inconsistent claims of different pressure groups on the national product." [16] Tobin later gracefully admitted that he had "been overoptimistic about the trade-off [between unemployment and inflation] and too skeptical of accelerationist warnings." [17]

Samuelson and Solow wrote in 1960 when inflation was low. The surge of world and U.S. inflation that started in the late 1960s has changed the picture. Inflationary expectations of market participants have become sensitized, and economists have been alerted to the danger of inflation. The change in outlook reached its climax in the theory of rational expectations. But we have seen that Keynes himself already recognized a change in climate in 1937 and urged a shift in policy to curb inflation without, of course, giving up the goal of full employment. Keynesian economists, on the other hand, have been slow to recognize the change and have been recommending expansionary policies in and out of season.

A dramatic example is provided by the Keynesians' complete misjudgment of the prospects of the British economy when the Thatcher government shifted the stance of policy. This was pointed out by *The Economist*, a bastion of Keynesianism, in an article entitled "UnKeynesian Britain." "When the [Thatcher] government raised taxes and cut public borrowing in the 1981 budget, 364 academic economists," mostly Keynesians, issued a manifesto predicting dire consequences. "Shortly thereafter recovery began," and the economy is still growing at a healthy pace despite the fact that the government has continued to shrink public sector borrowing. [18]

One of the 364 was Lord Kaldor. Two years later he still did not face the facts. In the introduction to his pamphlet *The Economic Consequences of Mrs. Thatcher* [19] he quotes the following passage from a famous speech by Keynes in the House of Lords on May 25, 1944, in which he defended the Bretton Woods agreement on the International Monetary Fund against its critics.

The experience of the years before the war has led most of us, though some of us late in the day, to certain firm conclusions. Three, in particular, are highly relevant to this discussion. We are determined that, in future, the external value of sterling shall conform to its internal value, as set by our own domestic policies, and not the other way round. Secondly, we intend to retain control of our domestic rate of interest, so that we can keep it as low as suits our own purposes, without interference from the ebb and flow of international capital movements, or flights of hot money. Thirdly, whilst we intend to prevent inflation at home, we will not accept deflation at the dictate of influences from outside. In other words, we abjure the instruments of the Bank rate and credit contraction operating through the increase in unemployment as means of forcing our domestic economy into line with external factors.[20]

Kaldor claims that this passage presents "the best account of the essential features underlying the consensus" that guided British economic policies of both labor and conservative governments in the postwar period. These essentially Keynesian policies, which have served the country so well, have been "completely repudiated" by the Thatcher government right from the beginning with disastrous consequences. Kaldor's theory calls for some critical comment.

To begin with, it is true that Britain and all other industrial countries, as well as most less-developed countries, experienced for about twenty years an almost unprecedented prosperity. Whether this was due to "enlightened Keynesian policies" is questionable; more on that below. But the "enlightened Keynesian policies" led to high, unsustainable inflation before Mrs. Thatcher came to power.

Mrs. Thatcher's policy certainly was not flawless. For example, it was a great mistake that early in the game she granted an excessive wage increase of over 20 percent to public sector workers. But the overall performance of the economy is by no means bad. Inflation has come down from 20 percent in mid-1979 to 5 percent in the past two years. The economy has been expanding since the middle of 1981 and continued to grow, albeit slowly, even during the 1982 recession in the United States, Japan, and Europe. Its growth rate was the highest among the countries in the European Community in 1983 and, according to the Organization for Economic Cooperation and Development, was likely to be one of the highest in 1984. Productivity in manufacturing increased at an annual rate of 6 percent in 1982 and 1983, and the prospects were good for 1984. Unemployment has remained high (about 12 percent), but employment has been increasing for about two years.

I now come to Keynes's statement. What he recommends is that Britain, while "preventing inflation at home," should under no circumstances allow deflation to be imported from abroad. The clear implication is that, if necessary, the exchange rate should be changed; in his words, "the external value of sterling should conform to the internal value."

Keynes's recommendation is the same that Thomas Willett and I made to the U.S. government when the dollar was weak in the 1970s: a policy of "benign neglect" of the balance of payments.[21]

Contrary to what Kaldor said, there is no conflict between that recommendation and the policy of the Thatcher government. This is precisely what the Thatcher government has done; it has abolished exchange control and allowed sterling to float in the foreign exchange market with a minimum of official interventions. Thus Kaldor's criticism completely falls to the ground.

It is interesting to recall that thirty-six years ago many Keynesians similarly misjudged the German economic "miracle," which started with the currency reform of 1948 and the simultaneous abolition of all controls by Ludwig Erhard after its early success had become apparent.[22] I cite one example: Thomas (Lord) Balogh predicted that the policies of Erhard "could not be sustained. The currency was reformed according to a wicked formula." It "helped to weaken the Trade Unions. . . . Their weakness may even inhibit increases in productivity, since large scale investment at high interest does not pay at the present low relative level of wages. In the long run the income pattern will become intolerable and the productive pattern unsafe." Balogh said that Dr. Erhard and his "satellite economists" were trying to discredit "enlightened Keynesian economic policies" and "to apply to real life an abstract obsolescent and internally inconsistent economic theory and certainly did not succeed." Balogh predicted alarming political consequences and pointed in "a final warning to the gains which the Soviet Zone of Germany has been able to record." Balogh was right in pointing out the extreme contrast between the economic ideas and policies prevailing in the Federal Republic of Germany and those in Britain under the labor government. The results, however, were the opposite of what Balogh and the other critics had predicted: German real GNP per capita has grown to almost twice that of Britain.[23] Hutchison also shows that German economic policies were similarly misjudged by American representatives of the "new economics," Walter Heller among them.

I offer a supplement to Hutchison's list of misjudgments of the

German revival of laissez-faire liberalism by advocates of central planning and comprehensive controls: in 1948, criticizing the view "that if, somehow, the German economy could be freed from material and manpower regulations, price controls and other bureaucratic paraphernalia, then recovery could be expedited," John K. Galbraith concluded, "there never has been the slightest possibility of getting German recovery by this wholesale repeal [of controls and regulations]."[24] Galbraith's paper abounds with predictions of the dire political and economic consequences of Erhard's dash for economic freedom. To quote Keynes: rarely has "modernist stuff gone wrong and turned sour and silly" so fast.

It should be recalled that in 1944, when he made the speech in the House of Lords, Keynes had completed a process of reconversion from protectionism, interventionism, and planning to economic liberalism. This seems to have been due largely to listening to Lionel Robbins, James Meade, Marcus Fleming, D. H. Robertson, and Redvers Opie.[25]

Actually, Keynes often changed his mind so fast that many of his followers could not keep pace. Thus Keynes had to defend the liberal Bretton Woods agreement against his followers who had become proponents of controls and central planning and were great admirers of the Nazi economic policy of Hjalmer Schacht. For example, a couple of months before his speech in the House of Lords, in a letter to the *Times*, Keynes replied to criticism by Thomas Balogh, who had urged controls: "Since we are not (so far as I am aware), except perhaps Dr. Balogh, disciples of Dr. Schacht, it is greatly to our interest that others should agree to refrain from such disastrous [Schachtian] practices."[26]

Kaldor also misinterprets Austrian developments. He writes: "Austria . . . adopted thoroughly Keynesian demand-management policies and enjoyed an uninterrupted prosperity with full employment ever since the early 1950s—with one of the highest growth rates in the world."[27]

To attribute the undoubted success of Austria's economic performance in the postwar period to the adoption of Keynesian policies is a widespread misconception, which is also shared by some Austrian economists. I have shown elsewhere that the Austrian policy is more appropriately described as Austro-monetarism than as Austro-Keynesianism.[28]

True, unlike the Swiss National Bank and the German Bundesbank, the Austrian National Bank does not pursue a strictly monetarist policy of setting monetary growth targets. But since Austria, very sensibly, pegs the Austrian schilling to the German mark, the

German Bundesbank in effect provides the monetarist basis for Austrian policy.

The basic *economic* reason why the performance of the Austrian economy was so much better after World War II than in the interwar period is that there was no deflation.[29] That is also true of the United States and all other industrial countries. We have seen that Kaldor completely misinterpreted the nature of the Great Depression; this explains why he missed the main reason of the "Austrian miracle," namely, that the deflationary mistakes of the 1930s were avoided.

To avoid misunderstanding, I repeat what I have said elsewhere: that the criticism of latter-day Keynesians does not mean that Keynes's recommendation of deficit spending in a deep depression when prices are falling and deflationary expectations prevail was wrong. On the contrary, it was quite right. This should also be acceptable to monetarists.[30]

The trouble is that many Keynesians, including Kaldor, do not understand that we do not live in a Keynesian world anymore. They do not realize the difference between a real deflation and depression and the transitional pains of disinflation. They speak of "the Volcker and Thatcher depression" and when sensitive commodity prices decline, they accuse the Federal Reserve of "deflationary" policies— joined by extreme supply-siders. Strange bedfellows!

Let me repeat: Keynes himself realized the change in climate in 1937; one year after the appearance of the *General Theory* he urged a shift in policy to fight inflation. We have to distinguish between Keynesian economics and the economics of Keynes.

The Third Stage. After criticizing Keynesians for past sins and misconceptions, I come to the *third* stage. Keynesians at long last have become aware that the economic climate has changed. As I have mentioned, James Tobin gracefully acknowledged that in earlier statements he had not given sufficient attention to the warnings of "accelerationists" such as William Fellner that inflation would accelerate because there is no permanent trade-off between unemployment and inflation.

My prime example, however, is the arch Keynesian Paul Samuelson. In his sparkling contribution to the Keynes Centenary Conference in Cambridge in 1983, he found that in the present world neither the "depression Keynesian model" of the *General Theory* nor "the market clearing new classical theory model" works well. He concludes: "If I had to choose between these two extreme archetypes, a ridiculous Hobson's choice, I fear that the one to jettison would have to be the Ur-Keynesian model"; and "people learn faster these days

35

and the easy Keynesian victories are long behind us."[31]

I myself have expressed the same idea by saying that today the world is closer to the classical position than to the Keynesian one. As mentioned, Keynes himself had already recognized in 1937 that the economic climate had changed when he argued that it was time to switch policy from fighting unemployment to curbing inflation.

Thus the third stage of Keynesian economics, exemplified by Samuelson, means that the Keynesians are at long last catching up with the view of the master. There are many examples of Keynes's quick turns that made it hard for many of his followers to keep pace. I cite one important example.

In a famous paper, "National Self-Sufficiency," Keynes wrote: "I was brought up to respect free trade as an economic doctrine which a rational and instructed person could not doubt. . . . As lately as 1923 I was writing that free trade was based on fundamental truths 'which, stated with their due qualifications, no one can dispute who is capable of understanding the meaning of the words.' "[32]

His views ten years later he summed up as follows: "I sympathize with those who would minimize rather than with those who would maximize, economic entanglement among nations. Ideas, knowledge, science, hospitality, travel—these are the things which should of their nature be international. But let goods be homespun whenever it is reasonably and conveniently possible."[33]

When Keynes became involved during the war in planning for postwar economic reconstruction, Bretton Woods, and trade policy, he at first strongly opposed the liberal trade policy proposed by the U.S. State Department. In a memo of October 1943 he wrote: "I am a hopeless skeptic about a return to 19th century laissez faire for which the State Department seems to have such a nostalgia. I believe the future lies with (I) state trading for commodities, (II) international cartels for necessary manufactures, and (III) quantitative import restrictions for non-essential manufactures."[34] Harrod writes: "In the preceding ten years he [Keynes] had gone far in reconciling himself to a policy of planned trade: these ideas had sunk deeply in. Even for him with . . . his power of quick adaptation, it was difficult to unlearn so much."[35] Another great admirer of Keynes, Lionel Robbins, wrote: "Even Keynes succumbed to the [then] current insanity. . . . A sad aberration of a noble mind."[36]

Keynes later changed his mind, but many of his followers, notably Nicholas (Lord) Kaldor and the new Cambridge school, have consistently followed the protectionist line.[37]

In his last years Keynes turned sharply against the protectionist-nationalist policies proposed by his erstwhile followers, who in the meantime had become his critics. It was these policies that he had in mind when he wrote in a famous posthumously published paper: "How much modernist stuff, gone wrong and turned sour and silly, is circulating in our system, also incongruously mixed, it seems, with age-old poison." He pleaded that the "classical medicine" should be allowed to work, that is to say, liberal trade policy, convertible currencies, and sound monetary and fiscal policies. "If we reject the medicine from our systems altogether, we may just drift on from expedient to expedient and never get really fit again."[38]

One final observation. It is misleading to contrast Keynes's macroeconomics with Marshallian, Walrasian, and other neoclassical microeconomics as Samuelson and other Keynesians do. This ignores the fact that Marshall and Walras have written extensively on money, banking, credit, and economic fluctuations. In other words, there exists a Marshallian and Walrasian macroeconomics.[39]

Of course they did not put their macroeconomics in the form of something like the "three-equation macro system of the *General Theory* type" that Samuelson finds so illuminating.[40] But that would not be hard to do. In fact, it has been done admirably by A.C. Pigou in his great book *Equilibrium and Employment*.[41] Pigou presents a truly *general* theory that comprises Keynes's *General Theory* as a very special case. The superiority of Pigou's work has been acknowledged by no less than the arch Keynesian Nicholas Kaldor.[42]

It is true that *Equilibrium and Employment* is of post-Keynesian vintage. Yet let me repeat what I wrote many years ago:[43] in 1950 Pigou published the text of two lectures, *Keynes' "General Theory": A Retrospective View*,[44] an eminently fair and generous reappraisal of the *General Theory*, which he had criticized rather bitterly soon after its appearance.[45] In his reappraisal Pigou writes: "When I wrote my *Employment and Equilibrium* in 1942, and again when I revised it recently, I had not read the *General Theory* for some time and did not realize how closely my systems of equations conform with the scheme of his analysis."[46]

On Pigou's statement, I commented in my 1962 paper: "It is, however, quite safe to say, it seems to me, that Pigou would not have written his *Employment and Equilibrium* without the Keynesian challenge. But it is equally clear that the new book, far from contradicting classical theory, constitutes a clarification and elaboration of Pigou's own pre-Keynesian 'classical' position."[47]

Notes

1. I repeat that Keynes himself soon changed his mind. Moreover, passages can be found in the *General Theory* that point in a different direction.

2. For a discussion of various possible causes of the Great Depression, see my paper *The World Economy, Money, and the Great Depression, 1919–1939* (Washington, D.C.: American Enterprise Institute, 1976).

3. Schumpeter's views are discussed in my paper *Schumpeter's Capitalism, Socialism, and Democracy after Forty Years*, American Enterprise Institute Reprint, no. 126 (Washington, D.C., October 1981). The paper appeared originally in Arnold Heertje, ed., *Schumpeter's Vision: Capitalism, Socialism, and Democracy after 40 Years* (New York: Praeger Publishers, 1981).

4. Raúl Prebisch, "Five Stages in My Thinking on Development," in World Bank, *Pioneers of Development* (Oxford: Oxford University Press, 1984), p. 175.

5. On the genesis of development economics, see the masterly introduction to the World Bank's *Pioneers in Development*, "The Formative Period," by Gerald M. Meier. Deepak Lal has subjected the theory to a scathing criticism in his hard-hitting classic *The Poverty of "Development Economics,"* Hobart Paperback 16 (London: Institute of Economic Affairs, 1983). I myself have tried a critical appraisal of development economics after putting it in historical perspective in "Liberal and Illiberal Development Policy: Free Trade like Honesty Is Still the Best Policy," which will be published by the World Bank in the second series of *Pioneers in Development*.

6. The great Keynesian and biographer of Keynes Roy G. Harrod took a different view. In his review of Milton Friedman and Anna J. Schwartz, *A Monetary History of the United States, 1867–1960* (Princeton, N.J.: Princeton University Press for National Bureau of Economic Research, 1963) in the *University of Chicago Law Review*, vol. 32, no. 1 (Autumn 1964), pp. 188–96, Harrod emphatically rejects the view held by many Keynesians "that the events of 1929–1933 proved the impotence of monetary policy" and asserts categorically that "monetary policy was not attempted in the United States in 1929–1933" (p. 196).

7. Friedman and Schwartz, *Monetary History*, p. 352.

8. Nicholas Kaldor, "The New Monetarism" (1970), reprinted in Kaldor, *Further Essays on Applied Economics* (New York: Holmes & Meier, 1978), pp. 18–19. Kaldor restated his theory in 1983 in "Keynesian Economics after Fifty Years," in David Worswick and James Trevithick, eds., *Keynes and the Modern World* (Cambridge: Cambridge University Press, 1983), esp. pp. 15–23.

9. Friedman and Schwartz, *Monetary History*.

10. Milton Friedman, in his paper "The Monetary Theory and Policy of Henry Simons," *Journal of Law and Economics*, vol. 10 (October 1967), p. 7, writes:

> There is clearly great similarity between the views expressed by Simons and by Keynes—as to the causes of the Great Depression, the impotence of monetary policy, and the need to rely extensively on fiscal policy. Both men placed great emphasis on the state of business

expectations and assigned a critical role to the desire for liquidity, [indeed] "absolute" liquidity preference under conditions of deep depression. . . . It was this that meant that changes in the quantity of money produced by the monetary authorities would simply be reflected in opposite movements in velocity and have no effect on income or employment.

See also Herbert Stein, *The Fiscal Revolution in the United States* (Chicago: University of Chicago Press, 1969); idem, "Early Memories of a Keynes I Never Met," *AEI Economist* (June 1983); and J. Ronnie Davis, *The New Economics and the Old Economists* (Ames: Iowa State University Press, 1971).

11. Arthur F. Burns, "An Economist's Perspective over 60 Years," *Challenge* (January–February 1985), p. 17.

12. On all that, see the three chapters on the Keynesian revolution in T. W. Hutchison's encyclopedic monograph *On Revolutions and Progress in Economic Knowledge* (Cambridge: Cambridge University Press, 1978), esp. chap. 6, "Demythologizing the Keynesian Revolution: Pigou, Wage Cuts, and *The General Theory*," pp. 175–200.

13. Paul Samuelson and Robert Solow, "Analytical Aspects of Anti-Inflation Policy," *American Economic Review*, vol. 50, no. 2 (May 1960), fig. 1, p. 192.

14. They refer to expectations in connection with the Phillips curve: "It might be that the low-pressure demand would so act upon wage and other expectations as to shift the curve downward in the longer run—so that over a decade, the economy might enjoy higher employment with price stability than our present-day estimate would indicate" (ibid., p. 193). But it is *deflationary* expectations, and it is described as a long-run phenomenon. Inflationary expectations surely are not a long-run phenomenon. This makes the absence of any reference to inflationary expectations all the more conspicuous.

15. Ibid., p. 185.

16. See his brilliant presidential address, James Tobin, "Inflation and Unemployment," *American Economic Review*, vol. 62 (March 1972), p. 13.

17. See James Tobin, "Comment of an Academic Scribbler," *Journal of Monetary Economics*, vol. 4 (1978), p. 622.

18. "UnKeynesian Britain," *The Economist* (London), February 2, 1984.

19. Nicholas Kaldor, *The Economic Consequences of Mrs. Thatcher* (London: Buckworth, 1983). *Speeches in the House of Lords, 1979–1982*, ed. Nick Butler, pp. 1–2.

20. Keynes's speech is reprinted in *Collected Writings of John M. Keynes*, vol. 26 (Cambridge: Cambridge University Press, 1980), p. 16.

21. See Gottfried Haberler and Thomas Willett, *A Strategy for U.S. Balance of Payments Policy* (Washington, D.C.: American Enterprise Institute, 1971). See also Gottfried Haberler, *U.S. Balance of Payments Policy and the International Monetary System*, American Enterprise Institute Reprint, no. 9 (Washington, D.C., January 1973).

22. On this see T. W. Hutchison, "Notes on the Effects of Economic Ideas on Policy: The Example of the German Social Market Economy," in *Zeitschrift*

für die Gesamte Staatswissenschaft: Currency and Economic Reform, West Germany after World War II, A Symposium, vol. 135 (September 1979) Tübingen, pp. 436–41.

23. Ibid., pp. 435–39; and Thomas Balogh, "Germany: an Experiment in 'Planning' by the 'Free' Price Mechanism," *Banca Nazionale Del Lavoro Quarterly Review* (Rome), vol. 3 (1950), pp. 71–102.

24. John K. Galbraith, "The Germany Economy," in Seymour E. Harris, ed., *Foreign Economic Policy for the United States* (Cambridge, Mass.: Harvard University Press, 1948), p. 95.

25. Keynes's exchange of letters and memoranda with the economists mentioned can be found in *The Collected Writings of John M. Keynes,* vol. 26.

26. Ibid., p. 9.

27. Kaldor, *Economic Consequences,* p. 5.

28. See my paper "Austria's Economic Development after the Two World Wars: A Mirror Picture of the World Economy," in Sven W. Arndt, ed., *The Political Economy of Austria,* a conference sponsored jointly by the American Enterprise Institute for Public Policy Research and the Austrian Institute (New York) (Washington, D.C.: American Enterprise Institute, 1982), pp. 64–76.

29. I underline "economic" to indicate that there were, of course, political reasons. They are discussed in my earlier paper but need not be discussed here.

30. On all this see my *World Economy, Money, and the Great Depression,* and *The State of the World Economy and the International Monetary System,* American Enterprise Institute Reprint, no. 92 (Washington, D.C., 1979).

31. See Paul Samuelson, "Comment," in Worswick and Trevithick, *Keynes and the Modern World,* p. 212.

32. John Maynard Keynes, "National Self-Sufficiency," *Yale Review* (Summer 1933), p. 755.

33. Ibid., p. 758.

34. Quoted in Roy F. Harrod, *The Life of John Maynard Keynes* (New York: Harcourt, Brace, 1951), pp. 567–68.

35. Ibid., p. 568.

36. Lionel Robbins, *Autobiography of an Economist* (New York: Macmillan, 1971), p. 156.

37. See Nicholas Kaldor, "The Nemesis of Free Trade" (1977), in Kaldor, *Further Essays in Applied Economics;* and idem, *Economic Consequences.*

38. See John Maynard Keynes, "The Balance of Payments of the United States," *Economic Journal,* vol. 61, no. 222 (1946), p. 186.

39. See Alfred Marshall, *Principles of Economics* on the one hand, and *Money, Credit and Commerce* and Marshall's *Official Papers* on the other. See also Leon Walras, *Elements d'Economie Politiques Pure,* definitive ed. (Paris, 1926), on the one hand, and his *Etudes d'Economie Politique Appliques* (Paris, 1898), on the other. It is worth noting that Marshall and Walras, along with acknowledged scholars like F.Y. Edgeworth, H.G. Pierson, and Irving Fisher, supported bimetallism (or symmetallism) in somewhat heretical opposition to the orthodoxy of the gold standard. This should help to dispel the myth

40

propagated by the Keynesians, with their limited historical horizon, that Keynes was the only reputable economist (apart from Silvio Gesell, Major Douglas, and scores of others whose views could be dismissed as those of monetary cranks) who offered a responsible opposition to the prevailing orthodoxy.

40. Samuelson, "Comment," p. 213.

41. A.C. Pigou, *Equilibrium and Employment*, 2d ed. (London: Macmillan, 1949, first published 1943).

42. See his review in the *Economic Journal* (December 1941).

43. See Gottfried Haberler, "The General Theory after Ten Years" (1946), and "Sixteen Years Later" (1962), both reprinted in Robert Lekachman, ed., *Keynes' General Theory: Reports of Three Decades* (London: St Martin's Press/ Macmillan, 1964), p. 294.

44. A.C. Pigou, *Keynes' "General Theory": A Retrospective View* (London: Macmillan, 1950).

45. See A.C. Pigou, book review, *Economica*, no. 1 (1937).

46. Pigou, *Keynes' "General Theory,"* p. 65.

47. Haberler, "Sixteen Years Later."

9
Growing Wage Rigidity

Wages have always been sticky, even before labor unions became as powerful as they are now. But there can be no doubt that in the post–World War II period they have become much more sticky than they were earlier.

The growing rigidity of wages and the resulting decline in the responsiveness of wages and prices to the decline in economic activity during recessions have been widely noted in the literature. I cite two papers that I found especially important, one by Phillip Cagan and the other by Jeffrey Sachs.[1]

Phillip Cagan concludes that "wholesale prices show a smaller decline in the recessions after 1948–49 than formerly" and that "there has clearly been a gradual decline in price response to recessions over the postwar period, except mainly for raw materials prices."[2] Sachs uses two methods to demonstrate the decreasing responsiveness of inflation to changes in aggregate demand, with special emphasis on wage behavior. The first approach follows Cagan's method and leads to the same conclusion for a longer period. A striking finding is that "for mild contractions, downward price flexibility seems to have ended with the pre–World War II period. For moderate and severe contractions, similarly, the response of wages and prices has fallen significantly since 1950."[3]

The second approach is described as an economic Phillips curve estimation. The result—that the short-run Phillips curve has become steeper—strongly supports the hypothesis of decreasing responsiveness of wages to declines in economic activity.

The causes of this development are fairly obvious. The spread of unionization of labor and the increased strength of labor unions, which largely go back to the New Deal legislation of the 1930s, are surely basic. That union wages are stickier than nonunion wages is notorious; that they seem to be stickier also on the upside of the cycle is amply overcompensated for by the sharp rise in the length of union contracts providing large wage increases for each year. The overlapping and leapfrogging of union wage contracts have greatly exacerbated the wage inflation caused by unions.[4]

In other industrial and industrializing countries the power of labor unions has also sharply increased, and so have wage push and what J. R. Hicks calls "real wage resistance." Naturally, the pattern and force of this development vary from country to country, depending on the structure of the economy, the history of the labor movement, and its alliance in many countries with political, mainly socialist, parties.

Without going into detail, I should mention that in most European countries a much larger percentage of the labor force is unionized than in the United States. In some countries— Austria and Sweden, for example—central organizations represent labor as a whole and allow it to speak with one voice.

Whether the existence of strong centralized organizations of labor as a whole or of a large part increases or decreases the dangers of inflationary wage push, compared with the decentralized U.S. system of essentially independent unions, is difficult to say. On the one hand, it increases the power of unions and their political influence. On the other hand, it eliminates leapfrogging, and the leaders of an all-embracing organization of labor may perhaps be assumed to be more responsible, more aware of the general good of the population as a whole than the leaders of independent unions.

International comparisons could throw some light on these questions, but I must confine myself to two remarks. First, international comparisons are complicated by the fact that union power also depends on the structure of the economy. It is well known, for example, that unions are more moderate in small countries where competition from world markets is strong because foreign trade plays a much greater role than in large countries. Second, Japan is a special case that merits close attention. The wages of Japanese workers are much more flexible than the wages of European and U.S. workers because Japanese workers receive a large part of their earnings in the form of bonuses whose size varies with profits. In recessions, when profits are low, wages and labor costs automatically decline. This is one of the reasons why unemployment is lower in Japan and why the economy rebounds more quickly from recessions than in most other industrial countries.

Another factor that derives its importance partly from the existence of powerful unions is the rise of Keynesianism with the resulting emphasis on antidepression and antirecession policy. This has a double inflationary effect: it reduces the price decline in the downswing of the business cycle and stiffens the resistance of workers and their unions to wage cuts, because they assume that unemployment caused by large wage boosts will not last long—in other words, that government policy will bail them out if they cause unemployment by excessive wage demands.

Other policies that strengthen union power and produce unemployment are minimum wages, especially since they are adjusted for inflation, and generous unemployment benefits and welfare payments. These measures reduce the responsiveness of wages and prices to recession by diminishing the incentive for individual workers to accept lower-paid jobs and for the unions to make wage concessions, especially if, as in some U.S. states, striking workers are eligible for unemployment benefits.

In a recent unpublished paper, Geoffrey H. Moore presented some very interesting figures that throw much light on the importance of large unemployment benefits for the size of unemployment and indirectly also for the cyclical unresponsiveness of wages.[5] The author finds that both in 1929, a boom year, and in 1982, a recession year, 58 percent of the population sixteen years old or older were employed. The 42 percent who were not working fall into two groups: the unemployed (not working but seeking work) and those who neither work nor seek work. The interesting finding is that, in 1929, 2 percent of the population were unemployed and 40 percent were not working or seeking work and, in 1982, 6 percent were unemployed and 36 percent were neither working nor seeking work.[6]

What explains the much higher unemployment percentage in 1982 than in 1929 when the employment rate was the same in both years? Moore asks the question the other way round: "What explains the increase in the desire to work on the part of the non-working population?" There are several reasons, but a major reason is that "in 1982 the unemployed were much better supported than in 1929. Fifty years ago none of the unemployed received unemployment insurance benefits from the government, since there was no insurance program." Moore says that "the average weekly benefit paid to the insured unemployed in 1982 was as high, in real terms, as the average weekly pay of all employed persons in 1929." Since "total compensation per worker employed in 1982 was roughly three times as high as in 1929, *after* allowing for inflation," average weekly unemployment benefits in 1982 amounted to roughly a third of the average compensation per worker.

This is a strong incentive to "remain as long as possible in the ranks of the unemployed." If "the unemployed in 1929 had had access to the benefits available to the insured unemployed today," unemployment would have been much higher and the percentage of nonworkers not seeking work lower than they were. I believe that Moore's paper also strongly supports the hypothesis, put forward above, that the published unemployment figures contain a sizable amount of spurious, voluntary unemployment.

Since this was written more than a year ago, there have been significant changes in the area under consideration. In the United States the unexpectedly vigorous cyclical expansion that started in November 1982 was accompanied by less wage pressure than earlier recoveries in the post–World War II period. Wage costs per unit of output did not rise much, and the inflation therefore remained relatively low. There is strong evidence that the relatively consistent policy of disinflation pursued in the United States in the past three years has improved the trade-off between unemployment and inflation. In a recent study Phillip Cagan and William Fellner put it this way: "In our appraisal, the data suggest an improved 'trade-off' for the past two years. By this we mean that during this period we obtained more disinflation per unit of economic slack (unemployment) than would be suggested by the same type of trade-off for the 1970s."[7]

It is probably too optimistic to conclude that inflation has definitely been stopped; it may well accelerate again if the expansion continues, and the support the anti-inflation policy has enjoyed from the strong dollar and the large trade deficit will not last forever. Moreover, unfortunately the U.S. labor picture is not uniformly bright. In two major industries, automobiles and steel, for example, powerful unions have managed to keep wages more than 50 percent higher than the average wage in U.S. manufacturing industries. This would not have been possible without strong support from the government through severe restrictions on imports of Japanese automobiles.

In its infinite wisdom the government has chosen the worst possible method of protection, the so-called voluntary restrictions imposed on foreign exporters. Any import restriction, tariff or nontariff, drives a wedge between the price inside and outside the country. Under an import tariff the price difference goes to the U.S. Treasury as a duty and so ultimately to the U.S. taxpayer. But under the method of "voluntary" export restraints forced on the Japanese firms, the price difference goes to foreign exporters. This means that foreign exporters receive a large subsidy at the cost of the U.S. consumer. Robert Crandall estimates that the Japanese automobile firms receive an annual subsidy of at least $2 billion a year from the United States because the price of Japanese cars has increased. The total "cost to the [American] consumer in 1983 was $4.3 billion plus additional losses in consumer welfare due to the constraint on the choice of cars. The cost per job saved [in the U.S. automobile] industry therefore was at least $160,000 per year." Crandall adds: "Employment creation at this cost is surely not worth the candle."[8] The same

45

vicious system is now being introduced for steel imports.

The system has a serious, corrupting side effect. Naturally foreign exporters, such as the Japanese automobile makers, quickly learn to like the system and no longer have any incentive to fight for free trade. They thus become accomplices of domestic protectionists, the U.S. automobile firms and the United Auto Workers (UAW). This means that free trade loses one of its most vocal supporters.

Yet the fact remains that the performance of the U.S. economy has been much better than expected. Especially remarkable and instructive is the contrast between Europe and the United States. The European economic picture is much less bright; the recovery from the recession started later and has been slower than in the United States; unemployment is higher; and there is more inflation in most European countries than in the United States.

What accounts for this contrast? There are basic structural differences, which have been very well presented by Stephen Marris, the former chief economic adviser of the Organization for Economic Cooperation and Development (OECD). I quote some salient facts described by Marris:

> European economies are in important respects less flexible than the American economy. . . . European workers are generally better protected against economic misfortune than their American counterparts. Collective agreements and government regulations give them more job security. But this makes it more difficult and expensive for European employers to lay off workers when demand weakens. And they are more reluctant to take on new workers when demand picks up, preferring instead to work overtime. Provisions for unemployment are also more generous in Europe. Laid-off workers have more time to look around for a new job. But, by the same token, this slows down the movement of labor from declining to expanding industries.
>
> Labor mobility is also inhibited in Europe by the greater rigidity of the *relative* wage structure between industries, occupations and regions. It is more difficult for employers in expanding industries to bid up wages to attract labor, or for laid-off workers in declining industries to bid down wages to get their jobs back.
>
> . . . The main culprit is the downward rigidity of real wages, coupled with the high taxes. . . . Europeans have been reluctant to swallow the rapid rise in taxation needed to finance the very rapid rise in public expenditure. Between

46

1960 and 1983 the ratio of general government expenditure to gross national product (GNP) in the European Community rose from 32 percent to 52 percent.

. . . In America the overall burden of taxation is lower, and real incomes seem to have adjusted more flexibly to the shocks of the 1970s. 20 million new jobs have been created in America since 1972. . . . Against this, there was a net *loss* of around 2.5 million jobs in the European Community over the same period. Compared with Europeans, Americans coming into the labor force have been more willing to accept whatever level of real wages was necessary to induce employers to hire them; in other words, to "price themselves" into jobs.[9]

To Marris's list of European handicaps I would add the following: the U.S. economy enjoys the tremendous advantages of a large free trade area of continental size and of private competitive enterprise in the fields of transportation, communications, and electric power.

The European Common Market was supposed to establish free trade among the members of the European Community (EC), but many impediments to the free movement of commodities still exist. Some members, notably France, have tight exchange control, which is a major obstacle to trade, although its purpose is ostensibly "merely" directed at capital transactions. Exchange control makes integration of financial markets impossible—a most serious handicap. Customs formalities and inspection at the border are still in place, and controllers and customs officials are very active to justify their existence.[10]

Equally important, European countries are burdened by the existence of national public monopolies in transportation, communications, and electric power. These state enterprises suffer in various degrees from bureaucratic inefficiencies and are impervious to international competition. Numerous nationalized industries also suffer from the same handicap.

Marris, however, is not satisfied with the structural explanation of the contrast between Europe and the United States. He insists that a basic difference between European and American macropolicies is equally if not more responsible. While the United States is running huge budget deficits, Europe's "recovery is being held back" by low structural deficits. In other words, European policies are not sufficiently expansionary ("Keynesian").

This I find unconvincing for two reasons. First, European macropolicies are by no means uniform. There is a sharp contrast, for example, between the two largest economies—France and West Germany. In France the Socialist government of François Mitterand has pursued Keynesian policy, running large budget deficits and, as a consequence, experiencing huge trade deficits, high inflation, and slow growth. West Germany has pursued a much more cautious policy; inflation is much lower than in France, and the West German economy has staged a fairly rapid recovery, although unemployment is still high by German standards.[11]

The second reason why Marris's theory is unconvincing is that, given the structural rigidities and immobility of labor as described by him, an expansionary ("Keynesian") macropolicy would quickly reignite inflation, as exemplified by France. This was pointed out by Helmut Schlesinger, vice-president of the Bundesbank. He made it clear that the Bundesbank would stick to its cautious policy, because accelerated inflation would soon be followed by a recession.

Notes

1. See Phillip Cagan, "Changes in the Recession Behavior of Wholesale Prices in the 1920's and Post–World War II," in *Explorations in Economic Research*, National Bureau of Economic Research, Occasional Papers, vol. 2, no. 1 (Winter 1975); and Jeffrey Sachs, "The Changing Cyclical Behavior of Wages and Prices: 1890–1976," *American Economic Review*, vol. 70, no. 1 (March 1980), pp. 78–90. Sachs's paper has extensive references to the literature. See also James E. Price, "The Changing Cyclical Behavior of Wages and Prices, 1890–1976: Comment," *American Economic Review*, vol. 72, no. 5 (December 1982); and Jeffrey Sachs's reply, "The Changing Cyclical Behavior of Wages and Prices, 1890–1976: Reply," *American Economic Review*, vol. 72, no. 5 (December 1982), pp. 1191–93.

2. Cagan, "Changes in Recession Behavior," pp. 54–55.

3. Sachs, "Changing Cyclical Behavior," p. 81.

4. On this point see the paper by John A. Taylor, "Union Wage Settlements during a Disinflation," *Working Paper No. 985* (Cambridge, Mass.: National Bureau of Economic Research, 1982), and the specialized literature quoted in the paper.

5. Geoffrey H. Moore, "Another 1929?" Center for International Business Cycle Research, Graduate School of Business, Columbia University, New York, June 3, 1983 (mimeographed).

6. The author explains that his figure for unemployment (6 percent in 1982) differs from the usually quoted official figure (10 percent) because he prefers to express unemployment as a percentage of the *total* population sixteen years old or older. The usually quoted figure is expressed as a percentage of the *labor force*, which is defined as the employed plus the unemployed. Those neither working nor seeking work (because of age or inability to work) are not considered part of the labor force. The difference in the definition does not affect the rest of the argument.

7. See Phillip Cagan and William Fellner, "The Cost of Disinflation, Credibility, and the Deceleration of Wages, 1982–1983," in William Fellner, project director, *Essays in Contemporary Economic Problems: Disinflation* (Washington, D.C.: American Enterprise Institute, 1984), p. 7.

8. Robert Crandall, "Import Quotas and American Industry: The Costs of Protectionism," *Brookings Review* (Summer 1984), p. 16. See also the excellent, comprehensive study by William R. Cline, *Exports of Manufactures from Developing Countries—Performance and Prospects for Market Access* (Washington, D.C.: Brookings Institution, 1984). Cline's conclusions are similar to mine. He estimates that about one-third of U.S. imports of manufactures are now under "voluntary" import restriction. (See also his article "Protectionism: An Ill Trade Wind Rises," *Wall Street Journal*, November 6, 1984.)

Since this was written, the Japanese have been informed by the U.S. authorities that the present regime of "voluntary" export quotas imposed on them would not be renewed after the expiration date of March 31, 1985. Unfortunately, the American consumer will not gain much from this "liberalization," for the Japanese firms will restrict exports for two reasons: first, it will give them larger profits; second, all-out competition in U.S. markets would surely unleash a major protectionist assault. The shift in U.S. policy was probably based on the assumption that the Japanese would not "abuse" the new freedom.

9. Stephen Marris, "Why Europe's Recovery Is Lagging Behind: With an Unconventional View of What Should Be Done about It," *Europe*, Magazine of the European Community (March/April 1984). Since this paper was written, an important, wide-ranging paper by Ambassador Arthur F. Burns, "The Economic Sluggishness of Western Europe" (delivered as the Dunlap Distinguished American Lecture, University of Dubuque, Iowa, September 5, 1984, to be published), has become available. Burns presents a thorough analysis of the structural handicaps of Europe as compared with the United States and vividly describes the excesses of the welfare state and the oppressive regulatory climate in many European countries.

10. True, tariffs and import quotas have largely been abolished between the members of the EC. But there has been a strong tendency to substitute more or less subtle administrative restrictions on intra-European trade. (See *The Economist* [London], June 23, 1984, p. 29, for details.)

Since this was written, *The Economist* has further discussed the subject (November 24, 1984, "Why Europe Has Failed" p. 13, and "Europe's Technology Gap," pp. 93–98). The articles describe in considerable detail the enormous benefits the United States derives from three facts: first, that its economy is a real free trade area of continental size with no restrictions or formalities at the state borders; second, that public utilities, airlines, railroads, and so on are in private hands, which ensures efficient, competitive large-scale production; and third, that safety and health regulations are uniform throughout the country. In stark contrast, Europe is sorely handicapped because the "common market" has failed dismally to establish real free trade; public utilities, airlines, and so on are in public hands, which means that output is far below the optimum; and safety, health, and other regulations vary from country to country. Thus Europe has been prevented from fully participating in

the biggest market-driven wave of economic development [the world] has known, detonated by an explosion of knowledge. By one estimate, nine times as much scientific knowledge has been generated since the second world war as mankind was able to produce in all its previous history. The amount of information in the world now doubles every eight years. Prosperity goes to countries that have a mechanism to put it to use. ("Why Europe Has Failed," p. 13.)

11. On the scope, speed, and prospects of the German recovery, see the statement by Helmut Schlesinger, vice-president of the German central bank. "Bundesbankpolitik auch 1985 für Wachstum bei Stabilität," *Deutsche Bundesbank Auszüge aus Presseartikeln*, no. 96 (December 12, 1984), pp. 1–2.

10
Some Further Comments on the Great Depression

I return to the Great Depression of the 1930s. We have seen that the New Deal policy of combining monetary and fiscal expansion with price- and wage-boosting measures caused stagflation and led to the short but very severe depression of 1937–1938.

The same mistake was committed by the Popular Front government under the premiership of Léon Blum that came to power in France in 1936. Its policy was modeled on the New Deal. The adverse effects on the French economy were compounded by the refusal of the new government to devalue the franc.

It is interesting to observe that the Socialist government of François Mitterrand, which came to power in May 1981, has been following in the footsteps of Blum and the New Deal. It, too, has combined wage- and price-boosting measures with monetary and fiscal expansion. The results are the same—stagflation and huge budget and balance-of-payment deficits.[1]

A very instructive contrast to the New Deal is provided by Nazi Germany. Roosevelt and Hitler came to power at about the same time fifty-two years ago. Each found his country in deep depression and immediately began expansionary measures.[2] Economic recovery in the United States, though long and pronounced, was marred by rising prices, which led to the interruption of the upswing, long before full employment was reached by the very severe though brief depression of 1937–1938. The German recovery, however, proceeded without interruption and reached substantially full employment within two or three years. Even more important, the price level in Germany remained remarkably stable for several years.

That the Nazis were concerned about the dangers of inflation is illustrated by the following true story. There was an influential Keynesian economist in the German Ministry of Economics who had advocated deficit spending for some time. In fact, there had been deficit spending even before Hitler. Under Hitler, however, the deficit became much larger. This man, Wilhelm Lautenbach (not a Nazi), was called in by Hitler, who asked: "Isn't this a little dangerous what we are doing? Are we not risking a serious inflation?" Lautenbach answered: "Mein Führer, you are a very powerful man, but there is one thing you cannot do: you cannot make inflation with 30 percent unemployment." What Hitler supposedly could not do, producing inflation in the midst of heavy unemployment, was achieved by the New Deal in the United States.

It is tempting to attribute the more rapid recovery in Germany than in the United States to massive expenditures on armaments. Heavy public spending there was indeed, but massive rearmament came only later. German public spending may have been comparatively larger than the American, but this would not explain the different price performances.

The main difference between the American and German recovery policies lies elsewhere: the New Deal combined spending with deliberate price and wage boosting. As a consequence, an exceptionally large part of the rising nominal GNP in the United States took the form of higher prices rather than larger output and employment. In Germany, in contrast, money wage rates remained fairly stable, although average annual earnings of labor rose rapidly in monetary and real terms along with rising output and employment, because unemployment disappeared and the workweek lengthened.

One could object that price controls and rationing make real wage figures under the Nazi regime meaningless. True, there were wage and price controls from the beginning of the Nazi dictatorship; and later, say, after 1936, when the rearmament boom came into full stride, scarcities, unavailabilities, and the deterioration of the quality of certain commodities made the official cost-of-living index increasingly unreliable. Fortunately, we have a careful study by Gerhard Bry.[3] Bry makes adjustments in the cost-of-living index to take account of the controls. His figures show that after about 1937 the official index understates the true rise in the cost of living. But for the earlier years (1933–1937) the corrections are minimal. There can, then, be no doubt about the great economic success of the Hitler regime. It is no exaggeration to speak of an economic miracle.[4] Another German economic miracle was the spectacular expansion of the German economy after World War II, which started with the currency reform in 1948 and the simultaneous abolition, at one stroke, of all price controls and rationing inherited from the war.

At this point Mancur Olson's well-known theory of the arteriosclerotic and arthritic afflictions of aging societies comes to mind.[5] Olson argues that the rise of what he calls "distributional coalitions,"

52

vested interests, and pressure groups tends to make modern economies more and more rigid and inflexible. But the process of rigidification is often halted or reversed by defeat in war or by revolutions that dissolve the pressure groups. He mentions the two German economic miracles as examples.[6]

Notes

1. Since this was written, the Socialist government has been forced to adopt a policy of relative austerity. The first effect was, unavoidably, a rise in unemployment. It is too early to judge the success of the new policy.

2. It is true that the German economy had a head start, for it had turned the corner in August 1932, six months before Hitler came to power. But that does not vitiate the comparison with the New Deal, because in the first six or seven months the German recovery was slow and the date of the trough of the U.S. depression, 1933, is not quite clear-cut; the depression has been described as "double bottomed," the first bottom occurring in 1932.

3. Gerhard Bry, assisted by Charlotte Boschan, *Wages in Germany, 1871–1945* (Princeton, N.J.: Princeton University Press for National Bureau of Economic Research, 1960), pp. xxvi, 486.

4. On Hitler's economic miracle, see Sebastian Haffner, *The Meaning of Hitler*. The reviewer in *The Economist* (London), October 20, 1979, describes this book as "a brief, incisive, adequate account of the monster which leaves no more worth saying to be said."

5. Mancur Olson, *The Rise and Decline of Nations: Economic Growth, Stagflation, and Social Rigidities* (New Haven, Conn.: Yale University Press, 1982).

6. He "predicts that with continued stability the Germans will accumulate more distributional coalitions, which will have an adverse influence on the growth rate" (ibid., p. 76).

11
Supply Shocks

Having discussed the wage factor, real wage resistance, and wage push, I now consider how supply shocks fit into the picture. The two oil shocks—the quadrupling of the price of crude oil in 1973 and the doubling of the price in 1979–1980—were and still are widely regarded as far the most important cause of two-digit inflation in 1974 and 1980–1981 and of the subsequent recessions.

This is surely a great exaggeration. The first oil shock was preceded and accompanied by a highly inflationary commodity boom, which was superimposed on an inflationary groundswell that encompassed the whole postwar period and went into high gear in the 1960s.[1] In the United States inflation was fueled by huge public borrowing to finance the escalating cost of the war in Vietnam and the equally costly Great Society programs of the Johnson administration and, of course, by accommodating monetary policy.

There is no doubt that the oil price rise had an inflationary effect, but the magnitude of the burden for the industrial countries has been greatly exaggerated. For the United States the additional oil import bill due to the first oil shock was about $20 billion a year. This is a large sum but not more than about 1.22 percent of the GNP at that time, or less than half the normal annual increase in GNP. It follows that a once-for-all small decrease of about 1.22 percent in the wage level, or more generally in money incomes, would have taken care of the problem; or, assuming that money wages were rigid downward, a once-for-all increase in the price level of about 1.22 percent would have solved the problem.[2] Now, an additional increase in inflation of 1.22 percentage points is of minor importance in a period of two-digit inflation.

For other industrial countries the oil levy was a greater burden than for the United States because they depend more heavily on imports. The jump in the oil import bill from 1973 to 1974 was 4.31 percent of GNP for Japan, 3.96 percent for Italy, 3.73 percent for the United Kingdom, and 2.17 percent for West Germany.[3] This was not a negligible burden, but it was not an intolerable one; for all countries of the Organization for Economic Cooperation and Development as a group it was less than one year's normal growth. Ideally, then, suspension of wage (income) growth for less than a year or a mild once-for-all rise in the price level would have taken care of the problem.

The conclusion that I draw is that if one wants to assign a major role in inflation and recession to the oil price rise, it must be done by stressing *indirect* effects; for example, by assuming what Hicks has called "real wage resistance," workers resisting not only money wage but also real wage changes, which would be brought about by widespread indexation of wages (and other incomes). There is surely much truth in this argument, and I shall return to the pivotal importance of the wage problem presently. But first a few words about the second oil shock.

The theory that supply shocks cause inflation and recession through real wage (income) resistance has been widely applied to the case of the second oil shock. I cite one example. Karl Otto Pöhl, president of the German Bundesbank, in a wide-ranging speech attributed "the present difficulties," high inflation and unemployment, "to the delayed effect of the second oil price shock," in the sense that "all segments of society defend their acquired income levels and living standards against the dictates of OPEC." He cited approvingly a statement of the European Economic Commission: "Sustained economic recovery cannot be secured unless in coming years labor and management accept pay increases substantially below the growth of productivity." With productivity growth near zero in most industrial countries, that implies that wages and other incomes have to be cut.[4]

Although in the first oil shock the OPEC crude oil price was quadrupled, in the second one it was "merely" doubled. For the United States the increase in the net oil import bill, the oil levy imposed by OPEC, amounted to about 0.52 percent of GNP. This can hardly be regarded as a major factor in the U.S. inflation or recession.

One could perhaps argue that the impact of the oil price rise was magnified by two facts: first, it impinged on a stagnating economy (low productivity growth); second, a further increase to keep up with U.S. and world inflation, which had not occurred after 1973, was widely expected. This argument is hardly convincing, however, in view of the fact that in the meantime market forces were at work to change the whole picture. The high price of oil induced conservation of energy and stimulated production of oil and other kinds of energy outside OPEC, so that the price trend has been sharply reversed.

I mentioned earlier that for other industrial countries the burden of the first oil shock was heavier than for the United States because

55

they depend more on oil imports. But the weight of the burden was not a crushing one. One of these countries, Britain, has joined the club of oil exporters without experiencing any marked relief of inflation.

The second oil shock was also more burdensome for other industrial countries than for the United States. In West Germany, for example, the increase in the levy from 1979 to 1980 was about 0.86 percent of GNP, compared with 0.52 percent for the United States. This factor can scarcely be assigned the major role in causing the West German inflation or recession—a conclusion supported by the fact that West Germany did not experience any notable improvement when the oil price tumbled in 1982.

Notes

1. See *International Financial Statistics, Supplement on Price Statistics*, no. 2 (International Monetary Fund), 1981.

2. If one accepts what might be called "the rational expectations" interpretation of the Keynesian theory—that workers do not accept a reduction in their real wage if it comes in the form of a reduction of the money wage because money wage reductions are never across the board—then the wage reduction imposed by the oil price increase would be an exception; for this reduction in wages clearly was across the board. An objection to this reasoning might be that there was change in relative wages after all, because wages in the domestic oil and oil-related industries might not go down. But this, surely, would be spinning things out too finely.

3. Based on Organization for Economic Cooperation and Development data. See *Economic Outlook*, no. 17 (July 1973), p. 56, table 21.

4. See Karl Otto Pöhl, "Remarks on the National and International Monetary Scenario," *Deutsche Bundesbank, Auszüge aus Presseartikeln* (Frankfurt am Main), no. 101, November 19, 1981.

12
The Wage Problem
Further Considered

It is now widely recognized that wage rigidity, real wage resistance, and real wage push are the most serious impediments to regaining price stability at high levels of employment and higher growth rates. In recent years more and more economists have come to the conclusion that a decisive and lasting recovery from the world recession requires a reduction in real wages and a substantial increase in profits to stimulate investment and growth. This implies a moderate decline in the share of wages in GNP; "wages," of course, include salaries. What is said about the adverse effect of wage rigidity and real wage resistance applies also to other incomes or prices that have been made rigid by government action, especially by indexation, ranging from farm supports to social benefits of various kinds.

I cite a few examples of this trend in thinking about wages. Two years ago a group of prominent German economists, several of them of the monetarist persuasion, issued a statement urging a temporary wage freeze to let inflation bring down real wages. The plea was not heeded; wages continued to rise, and unemployment has reached the two-digit level.

Herbert Giersch, an author with monetarist leanings, has argued in several important articles that most industrial countries, especially in Western Europe, suffer from excessively high real wages and excessively low profits.[1] Professor Giersch's diagnosis has been confirmed by an expert report to the European Commission (EC) in Brussels, which was cited in an article in the *Wall Street Journal*.[2] The report concludes that European businesses have invested too much in labor-saving machines and "that prosperity might be better served by employing human beings even if there is a machine that can do the same job [more cheaply]. Europe has actually gotten a poor return from heavy capital spending over the past decade." Europe invested 20 percent of GNP, compared with 16 percent in the United States. The report concludes that wages are too high; it should be added that interest rates are too low, and that induces an excessive substitution of capital for wages.[3]

The theme has been taken up by *The Economist* of London in two important articles.[4] *The Economist* asks for a substantial cut in *money* wages to bring about an increase in profits for the purpose of stimulating investment, growth, and employment. Predictably, this has shocked many of *The Economist*'s Keynesian readers.[5]

The main argument against cutting money wages as a recovery measure is that it reduces total spending by reducing the money income of labor and is thus a deflationary factor that intensifies the recession. This argument is fallacious, however, and rests on a misunderstanding of what a wage cut is supposed to achieve. The purpose would not be to reduce effective demand (nominal GNP); if such a reduction is necessary, it should be done by monetary-fiscal measures. The purpose of cutting money wages would be to boost profits and stimulate investment, employment, and growth by making labor more competitive with robots and other machines; in other words, with capital. If hourly wage rates are cut by 10 percent, that does not necessarily mean that the wage bill and the spending power of labor are reduced. If the elasticity of demand for labor is greater than unity (as it almost certainly is in the medium run), employment (in hours) will rise by more than 10 percent, and the wage bill and spending will rise too. True, if employment rises by less than 10 percent, labor incomes will decline, but that does not mean that total incomes and spending will also decline. A shift to profits will stimulate investment, employment, and growth. This tendency could be assisted by monetary expansion, for the reduction of unit labor cost would reduce the inflationary danger of easier money.

What these three statements of the problem have in common is that they assume that market forces will, in due course, bring about the necessary restructuring of the economy to achieve substantially full employment, provided a moderate cut in the wage level is achieved and macroeconomic levers are set right. The first of the two articles in *The Economist* cited above brings that assumption out very clearly. It argues that entrepreneurs would find hundreds of ways of substituting labor for capital if labor costs were reduced, just as they found ways to substitute capital for labor when wages went up.

This optimistic conclusion will be challenged by the "structuralists." Thus in the 1930s it was widely believed that part of the unemployment problem was that labor-saving inventions had reduced the demand for labor or that the "structure of production" had been distorted in some other way. In other words, it was argued that a large part of unemployment was technological and structural, requiring large-scale reallocation of factors of production—a time-consuming, painful process. There can be no doubt that subsequent developments were entirely at variance with that structuralist theory. Experience has shown that as soon as deflation was stopped, the huge structural distortions that had been diagnosed by theorists during the depression shriveled as quickly as they had surfaced earlier. What was called "secondary deflation" turned out to be a much more important cause of high unemployment than structural distortions.[6] In other words, there would have been some "structural" unemployment even if there had been no deflation (no contraction of the money stock), but the great bulk of unemployment was "Keynesian," or monetarist, not structural or "Hayekian."

Extreme structuralist views can be heard again today. It is said that robots and other "smart" machines have put human labor in the same position as horses when tractors came into widespread use. This is, however, a very misleading analogy. Tractors replaced not only horsepower but also manpower. But unlike horses, human labor could be shifted to producing tractors.

This is not to deny the possibility that technological progress may require reallocations of factors of production, which may cause some structural unemployment and at least a temporary decline of labor's share of GNP until the transfer and retraining of labor have been carried out. As we have seen, a modest decline of the share of labor in the national product is probably required at the present time. But it is most unlikely that a large permanent reduction of the marginal productivity of labor, an intolerable drop in the real wage, and a massive decline of the share of labor (and salaries) would occur, as the analogy with the horses suggests. As far as we can tell, the share of labor in the national product has remained remarkably stable over the long pull—apart from cyclical fluctuations—despite the tremendous technological changes, including mechanization and automation, that have occured since the industrial revolution in England.

I conclude that the present-day forecasts of the disaster that will befall us unless radical reforms, involving massive redistribution of income to spread work, are undertaken will turn out to be totally unfounded. These forecasts will share the fate of earlier gloomy prophecies, which have regularly made their appearance in periods of depression, from those underlying the Luddite movement in the early nineteenth century to the most famous one, Karl Marx's theory of the increasing misery of the working classes—prophecies that were completely disproved and discredited by subsequent developments.

Notes

1. See Herbert Giersch, "Arbeit, Lohn und Productivität," *Weltwirtschaftliches Archiv*, vol. 119 (1983), pp. 1–18, and the empirical literature quoted there; and idem, "Prospects for the World Economy," *Skandinaviska Enskilda Banken Quarterly Review* (Stockholm) (1982), pp. 104–10. He recently restated his views in "Perspektiven der Weltwirtschaft" [Perspectives for the World Economy], Kieler Discussion Paper (Kiel, 1984) (mimeographed).

2. "Machines Blamed for Europe's Joblessness," *Wall Street Journal*, November 19, 1984.

3. The theory that in some European countries real wages are too high has received its most thorough econometric test in an article by Jacques R. Artus, "The Disequilibrium Real Wage Rate Hypothesis: An Empirical Evaluation," *IMF Staff Papers*, vol. 31, no. 2 (June 1984), pp. 249–302. The author concludes:

> As far as the manufacturing sector is concerned, there are indeed strong reasons to believe that in France, the Federal Republic of Germany, and the United Kingdom the real wage rate is too high, in the sense of being incompatible with high employment. In particular, in these three countries we did not find any evidence that a large part of the actual increase in the share of labor costs in value added is warranted by long-run changes in production techniques, in the price of energy, or in the relative availability of labor and capital (p. 292).

4. "Work on a Pay Cut," *The Economist* (London), November 27, 1982, pp. 11–12; and "Wage Cuts," *The Economist* (London), December 18, 1982, pp. 14–15.

5. For samples of the dissenting letters, see *The Economist*, December 18, 1982. *The Economist* rightly argues that Keynes, if he were alive, would support its position and not that of its critics. It is one thing to say, as Keynes did in the 1930s, that a deflationary spiral should be stopped by expansionary measures rather than by wage reductions and an entirely different thing to urge in a period of persistent, severe stagflation that the level of money wage rates must not be touched. As I have mentioned, one year after the publication of his *General Theory* Keynes urged a shift in policy to fight inflation. We have to distinguish between Keynesian economics and the economics of Keynes.

6. "Secondary" meant that the primary cause was some large distortions, which were supposed to have triggered the deflationary spiral. This is certainly a possible explanation, keeping in mind what Milton Friedman and Anna J. Schwartz say in their classic *A Monetary History of the United States, 1867–1960* (Princeton, N.J.: Princeton University Press for National Bureau of Economic Research, 1963), p. 419:

> Small events at times have large consequences . . . there are such things as chain reactions and cumulative forces. It happens that a liquidity crisis in a unit fractional reserve banking system is precisely the kind of event that can trigger—and often has triggered—a chain reaction. And economic collapse often has the character of a cumula-

tive process. Let it go beyond a certain point, and it will tend for a time to gain strength from its own development as its effects spread and return to intensify the process of collapse. Because no great strength would be required to hold back the rock that starts a landslide, it does not follow that the landslide will not be of major proportions.

Friedman and Schwartz refer specifically to "a liquidity crisis in a unit fractional reserve banking system." Clearly, a sufficiently serious distortion can also be the trigger.

13
Policy Implications

The policy implications of my analysis are straightforward. Before going into details, I make two general observations.

First, my emphasis will be on anti-inflation policy, because this is the major macroeconomic problem confronting the world, especially the industrial countries, at the present time. This assertion should not be interpreted, however, as denying that the *real* economy, output, employment, and growth are intrinsically much more important than price stability. It rather reflects the conviction, which we have learned from long, painful experience, that chronic inflation is no cure for unemployment. There is no long-run trade-off between unemployment and inflation. In technical terms, the short-run Phillips curve shifts up and becomes steeper and steeper when inflation continues.

To elaborate a little: the global recession, the severest in the post–World War II period, from which the world economy is emerging at the present time was caused when the major industrial countries, led by the United States, were forced to step on the monetary brake after many years of inflationary abuse. It is simply impossible to wind down an entrenched inflation without creating transitional unemployment—in other words, without a more or less serious recession.[1]

The *second* general observation is something I said earlier: that inflation, including stagflation, is a monetary phenomenon in the sense that it cannot be stopped without monetary restraints, a reduction of monetary growth. In a sense monetary restraint is not only a necessary condition for bringing down inflation but also a sufficient condition. It is sufficient in the sense that it can bring down inflation irrespective of union strength, cost-raising policies of the government, or the size of the government budget deficit.

As an example, recall the cost-raising policies of the New Deal in the 1930s, which produced cost inflation and caused an exceptionally large part of the rising demand (nominal GNP) to go into prices rather than into quantities. Inflation was stopped abruptly by monetary restraint, which caused a short but very severe depression from March 1937 to June 1938. As measured by the consumer price level, inflation tumbled from 4.6 percent in the March 1936–March 1937 period to −3.2 percent during the depression. But in thirteen months industrial production slumped 32.4 percent, and unemployment rose from 11 percent to 20 percent.

The common sense of the matter is that the greater the resistance to wage and price reductions on the part of unions, other pressure groups, and the government and the stronger the cost-raising measures of the government, the stronger must monetary restraint be to bring down inflation. The greater the transitional unemployment and output loss of the anti-inflation policy, the harder it is politically to carry disinflation to a successful conclusion.

A loose fiscal policy (that is, large budget deficits) does not make it impossible to stop inflation by tight money. If the deficits exceed a certain limit, however, the side effects make it politically and economically harder to stop inflation. What the critical size is need not be discussed here. Suffice it to say that it largely depends on the volume of savings available for productive private investment. It stands to reason that large deficits drive up interest rates and crowd out productive private investment. The political pressure on the central bank to bring down interest rates by expansionary measures is bound to increase. Moreover, the rate of growth of real GNP will decline if productive private investment is reduced. As a consequence, a larger reduction in monetary growth will be required to achieve price stability.

The policy conclusions are straightforward. For best results monetary policy should be supplemented and assisted by an appropriately tight fiscal policy and by microeconomic measures to make the economy more flexible to improve the trade-off between prices and quantities. Thus in a period of expansion, such as the New Deal period in the 1930s or the present recovery, the aim would be that the expansion in aggregate demand (nominal GNP) be reflected in rising quantities rather than in rising prices. In a period of disinflation, however, the necessary decline in nominal GNP growth should be reflected in prices rather than quantities (output and unemployment).

This general prescription has been discussed and spelled out, in roughly similar ways, under different headings. What gave rise to these discussions was the poor performance of most industrial economies in the late 1970s and early 1980s: stagnant output and high unemployment, even in nonrecession years. This experience has shaken confidence in exclusive reliance on demand management and has spurred the search for an explanation of the slowdown and for a cure. One answer has been that what is required is the adoption of ''adjustment policies'' to speed up the economy's adjustment to

63

changing conditions. Adjustment policies have been the theme of two important reports, one by the General Agreement on Tariffs and Trade (GATT) and the other by the Organization for Economic Cooperation and Development (OECD).[2]

Advocates of incomes policy say that this is exactly what incomes policy is all about. The trouble is that incomes policy means different things to different people. It is often interpreted as more or less comprehensive wage and price controls. In that form incomes policy must be rejected. Wage and price controls are too crude; they deal with symptoms only, distort the economy, and have never worked.[3]

I have distinguished between Incomes Policy I and Incomes Policy II. The former is defined as more or less comprehensive wage and price control, including tax-oriented policy (TIP) and wage and price freezes. The latter is a bundle of measures designed to move the economy closer to the competitive ideal.

Before indicating what measures I have in mind, let me say a few words on what is now often called, especially in Europe, "supply-oriented economic policy." This is largely the same as what I call Incomes Policy II and adjustment policies, a bundle of measures designed to make the economy more flexible and efficient by breaking down impediments to competition in commodity and labor markets that would result in increasing supplies all around. Obviously the composition of the bundle must be assumed to change over time and to vary from country to country, depending on the structural problems confronting each country

Two more general remarks are required before I discuss the concrete measures that should be taken. First, supply-oriented policy is a much broader concept than, and must be distinguished from, supply-side economics, which flourishes in the United States but is hardly known in Europe.[4]

Second, adjustment policies and supply-oriented policies (or supply-side economics for that matter) should not be regarded as alternatives to or antitheses of "demand-side economics" (demand management). They are complements, not substitutes. And demand management should not be equated with Keynesianism. It is, after all, the task of monetary policy to keep aggregate demand on an even keel, so as to avoid inflationary or deflationary spirals. This statement is independent of the precise rule that monetary policy follows to achieve its goal.

Notes

1. The true nature of the U.S. and world recession has been widely misinterpreted, by economists as well as noneconomists, as something much more serious than a reaction to disinflation. Grandiose schemes of coordinated global reflation to "save the world economy" have been proposed by well-known statesmen and economists, not to mention the shrill demands for a "new economic order" and massive "resource transfers" from North to South emanating from the recent conference in Belgrade of the United Nations Conference on Trade and Development (UNCTAD). The vigorous recovery of the U.S. economy (despite the "overvalued" dollar and the large U.S. trade deficit) and the emergence of the world economy from the recession, which seems to have been sparked by the U.S. recovery, contradict all the pessimistic forecasts. For further details see my paper "The International Monetary System in the World Recession," in William Fellner, project director, *Essays in Contemporary Economic Problems: Disinflation* (Washington, D.C.: American Enterprise Institute, 1984).

A striking example of excessive pessimism based on misinterpretation and misinformation is a widely quoted statement by Helmut Schmidt, former chancellor and minister of finance of West Germany. At a World Forum sponsored by the American Enterprise Institute in Vail, Colorado, on August 28, 1983 (*New York Times*, August 29, 1983), Schmidt said that unemployment in West Germany is about as high as in 1931, two years before Hitler came to power; he mentioned the figure of 3 million. Actually, unemployment in Germany is 2.2 million now and was over 4 million in 1931. Moreover, a comparison of numbers of unemployed is misleading because of large territorial changes and profound changes in the labor force (such as female workers and guest workers). What is relevant for judging the severity of the depression is the unemployment rate as a percentage of the labor force. In 1931 unemployment was more than three times as high as now—34.3 percent against 8.9 percent. (See Walter Galenson and Arnold Zellner, "International Comparison of Unemployment Rates," *The Measurement and Behavior of Unemployment* [Princeton, N.J.: Princeton University Press for the National Bureau of Economic Research, 1957], p. 455.)

2. See General Agreement on Tariffs and Trade, *Adjustment, Trade and Growth in Developed and Developing Countries*, GATT Studies in International Trade, no. 6 (Geneva, 1978); and Organization for Economic Cooperation and Development, *Positive Adjustment Policies: Managing Structural Change* (Paris: OECD, 1983).

3. This negative judgment also applies to the so-called tax-oriented incomes policy (TIP), which substitutes tax incentives and deterrents for absolute controls. TIP would be an administrative nightmare; for that reason it has never been tried. Wage and price "freezes" have been tried but never with success. For a more detailed criticism of these policies, see my book *Economic Growth and Stability: An Analysis of Economic Change and Policies* (Los Angeles: Nash Publishing, 1974); and Gottfried Haberler, "Reflections on the U.S. Trade Deficit and the Floating Dollar," in William Fellner, project director,

Contemporary Economic Problems 1978 (Washington, D.C.: American Enterprise Institute, 1978), pp. 233–38.

4. Let me make my position clear: supply-siders have a valid point when they say that high taxes, especially high marginal tax rates, have become a drag on incentive to work, to save, and to invest. But it is dangerously overoptimistic to assume, as supply-siders do, that tax reductions all by themselves will turn the economy around almost overnight and that the resulting increases in output will take care of even large budget deficits. Supply-oriented policy will include, as one element among many others, removal of tax impediments to work, save, and invest.

14

Specific Measures of Incomes Policy II, Alias Supply-oriented Policy

Supply-oriented policy is, of course, a vast area. Only a few basic facts and principles can be dealt with here.

To bring the economy closer to the competitive ideal, all forms of monopoly and restriction of trade should be attacked. It will be convenient to deal separately with business or industrial monopolies (including oligopolies and cartels), with labor monopolies (labor unions), and with the government.

The rules of conduct of business and labor monopolies are rather different, but they have this in common: they restrict supply, keep prices and wages higher than they would be under competition, and slow productivity growth. In my opinion, in the present-day world, labor unions are much more powerful, present a greater danger for price stability and full employment, and are much more difficult to deal with than business monopolies.

Compared with labor unions, private business or industrial monopolies are really not much of a problem, except in the area of public utilities. The most effective antimonopoly policy, which is at the same time easy to carry out from the economic and administrative point of view (though not politically), is free trade. Given the enormous growth of world trade, especially of manufactures, in the past forty years, the great advances in the technology of transportation, communications, and information, and the emergence of new industries in scores of developed and developing countries, few if any monopolies would survive in a free trade world, outside the area of public utilities, where prices are under public control.

Free trade policy must, of course, be interpreted broadly. It would include not only the phasing out of tariffs, import quotas, and exchange control but also the elimination of administrative protectionism, the so-called voluntary restrictions imposed on foreign exporters (often called "orderly marketing agreements") and the taking over of noncompetitive firms by the government and operating them with great losses at the expense of the taxpayer. A policy along these lines would not require any new government bureaus or larger bureaucracies. On the contrary, it would reduce government activities, shrink the public sector, and lighten the tax burden.

I now come to the problems of the labor market. To begin with, liberalizing internal and international trade would go a long way toward curbing the monopoly power of labor unions. Unions know or quickly find out that striking against world markets is risky. That is why labor unions in small countries where the international sector is a large fraction of the economy are usually much more reasonable and moderate than in large countries where the international sector is small.

This is strikingly illustrated by two recent developments, although they do not come from the international area: the deregulation in the United States of the trucking and airline industries. Until recently the two industries were tightly regulated by two huge federal bureaucracies. The dismantling of the controls is equivalent to the introduction of internal free trade.

Deregulation—internal free trade—changed the structure of the two industries dramatically. New, largely nonunionized firms—regional airlines—with lower costs and dynamic management sprang up, providing better and much cheaper service to the public. In both cases the power of the unions was sharply reduced. The wage rates and wage costs of the new airlines are much lower than those of the old ones. It is not surprising that the unions are strongly opposed to deregulation. The union of the airline pilots went so far as to threaten a general strike to force the government to restore tight regulations, to protect the exorbitant salaries that they were able to obtain under the former system.

It is interesting to ask the question, What would happen if the competition for the established airlines had come from abroad, rather than from domestic sources? Surely the resistance to deregulation would have been much stronger.[1]

Finally, I mention a few specific measures that would promote the efficiency of the labor market, reduce the monopoly power of labor unions, increase the productivity of labor, and thus lead to a rise in real wages. Minimum wage laws, for example, exist in many countries, France and the United States among them. Legal minimum wages serve no useful purpose. On the contrary, it has been shown conclusively that in the United States the legal minimum wage is largely responsible for the shockingly high unemployment (up to 40 percent) among teenagers, especially black ones. These young people are thus deprived of the on-the-job training so important to their future careers. Minimum wage laws should be abolished.[2]

In the United States laws such as the Davis-Bacon Act obligate the government to buy only from firms that pay union wages. Given the large size of the public sector and the huge volume of government purchases, ranging from paper and pencils to trucks and turbines, these laws add considerably to the monopoly power of unions—and to the size of the government budget. Such laws, too, should be abrogated.[3]

Having discussed private monopolies of business and labor and what to do about them, I must say a few words about the role of the government. Actually, the government is the worst offender. The list of its misdeeds is very long indeed.

To begin with, public policy is largely responsible for the power of private monopolies. We have seen that without protection from imports few if any private monopolies, oligopolies, or cartels would exist outside the public utility area, where prices are in any case controlled. In fact, in most countries public utilities, postal services, railroads, and telephone and telegraph services are government monopolies. Prices in this area are notoriously rigid, and in many countries these public enterprises operate inefficiently and add substantially to the deficit of the government budget, crowding out productive private investment. In addition, the enormous burdens of the welfare state and the overregulation of industries contribute to the tax burden, blunting incentives to work, save, and invest.

When producers are too numerous to organize themselves to cut production and raise prices, the government steps in and does for them what unions do for their members. Farm price supports are the most important though not the only example. In the United States and even more in the European Community (Common Market), farm price supports have become a heavy burden on the government budget and a source of inflation.[4]

There are thus infinite opportunities for adjustment policies and supply-oriented policies to improve the performance of the economy—to make it more efficient and competitive and speed up the rate of productivity and GNP growth.

Notes

1. The large size of the U.S. market, which makes possible competition in industries that are subject to increasing returns to scale, is a great national asset. Few other countries enjoy that advantage.

2. For an exhaustive discussion of these problems, see Simon Rottenberg, ed., *The Economics of Legal Minimum Wages* (Washington, D.C.: American Enterprise Institute, 1981); and Masanori Hashimoto, *Minimum Wages and On-the-Job Training* (Washington, D.C.: American Enterprise Institute, 1981).

3. See John P. Gould and George Bittlingmayer, *The Economics of the Davis-Bacon Act: An Analysis of Prevailing Wage Laws* (Washington, D.C.: American Enterprise Institute, 1980).

4. Though excessively lavish and a heavy burden on the budget, the U.S. policy of subsidizing agricultural production is less objectionable than the EC policy, because the United States clearly has a great comparative advantage in agriculture over Europe.

15
Industrial Policy

Finally, I must add a word on a new development that would greatly increase the government's involvement in the economy. A strong movement is under way to add yet a new dimension to economic policy. What I have in mind is the urgent demand, which has strong support in Congress, that the United States develop an "industrial policy," that it can no longer rely as in the past on the private Schumpeterian entrepreneurs to introduce new products and new methods of production, to transform the economy and thus lift it to higher and higher levels.

It is all a little vague. The call for an industrial policy is in response to the slowdown of economic growth in all industrial countries since the 1970s. It can thus be regarded as a new version of the theory of secular stagnation that flourished during the Great Depression of the 1930s. Of course, today no one would argue, as the proponents of the theory of secular stagnation did, that we are suffering from oversaving, that is, an excess of saving over investment with deflationary consequences. Still, it is said, as in the 1930s, that investment has declined partly because of a lack of entrepreneurship, an absence of technological breakthroughs, and a slowing down of technological progress.

It is hardly necessary to point out that the theory of a slowdown of technological progress has turned out to be totally false. In fact, there has been a veritable explosion of scientific and technological advances providing an enormous mass of investment opportunities. *The Economist* recently said that there has been

> the biggest market-driven wave of economic development [the world has known], detonated by an explosion of knowledge. By one estimate, nine times as much scientific knowledge has been generated since the second world war as mankind was able to produce in all its previous history. The amount of information in the world now doubles every eight years. Prosperity goes to countries that have a mechanism to put it to use.[1]

The United States has been able to take full advantage of this opportunity because it is blessed with a domestic free trade area of continental size and because productive, competitive private enterprise is in charge of transportation, communications, and electric power. In sharp contrast Europe is severely handicapped by fragmented markets—despite the existence of the "Common Market"—and the existence of public monopolies in transportation, communications, and so on, and many nationalized industries. These state enterprises suffer from bureaucratic inefficiencies and are impervious to competition.

Yet the proponents of industrial policy speak of a lack of entrepreneurial vigor. Symptoms or aspects of this are said to be a declining trend in expenditures on research and development and an increasing share of lawyers and accountants among corporate executives, reflecting a decreasing share of businessmen (entrepreneurs).

I cite some striking examples of lively entrepreneurial activity that contradicts the theory of the lack of entrepreneurial talent. The economic rejuvenation of New England is one example. In the past two decades or so the economy of the region has undergone a basic transformation. It has emancipated itself from the traditional, obsolescent textile and shoe industries. Their place has been taken by high-technology industries—micro-ball bearings, computer hardware, and the like. These industries are composed of numerous small and medium-sized firms.[2]

The same thing has happened on an even larger scale in the West. The spectacular development of high-technology industries in "Silicon Valley" in California is also a classic example of competitive capitalism. It has been described in *The Economist* as "an engine of growth that is the envy and obsession of the rest of the world," including Japan.[3] It is the work of private enterprise, which makes nonsense of the theory that the United States needs a new industrial policy run by the government.

It will perhaps be argued that the high-technology industries, electronics and the rest, have been stimulated by the public sector, by defense and aerospace requirements. Of course, private enterprise did respond to public sector demands and received large research grants for special tasks. But defense and aerospace are not the most productive uses for entrepreneurial activity, although there may be productive byproducts; they do not by themselves satisfy human needs. There is, however, no reason to doubt that in the absence of these public demands, truly productive outlets for entrepreneurial ingenuity and energies would be found. It is, of course, true that a sudden collapse of public demand, resulting, for example, from a disarmament agreement with the Soviet Union, would cause serious transitional difficulties.

Still another example of lively entrepreneurial activity is provided by the deregulation of the trucking and airline industries. This was immediately followed by the creation of new firms in both industries.

The growing role of lawyers and accountants in corporate board rooms and elsewhere in the economy is easily explained by the ever-tighter web of government regulations and high tax rates. These divert entrepreneurial and legal talents to the unproductive task of coping with regulations and evading and minimizing taxes.

Proponents of an industrial policy have recommended a range of measures that would come under the umbrella of industrial policy. These include imposing a broad consumption tax, setting up tripartite boards of representatives of labor, management, and the government to help manage firms and industries, and establishing a central planning authority.

What they have in common and what constitutes the core of industrial policy is that some special government agencies should identify industries with a high "growth potential" and help them along with tax breaks, subsidies, research grants, special cheap loans, and import restrictions. This is a revival, or rather a perversion, of the old infant-industry argument for protection. Alexander Hamilton, the father of infant-industry protection in the United States, is often cited as an early practitioner of industrial policy. But although the classical theorists of infant-industry protection, including Hamilton, John Stuart Mill, Alfred Marshall, and others, were careful to restrict the applicability of the policy to "industrial infants" (what we now call less-developed or developing countries), the modern version applies it to highly developed countries. "Senile-industry protection" would be a better description of the proposals of the modern proponents of an industrial policy.

Actually, U.S. industry cannot be described as senile. The whole postwar development has been astounding. I have mentioned the economic rejuvenation of New England as a striking example of entrepreneurial development. The strong cyclical recovery of the U.S. economy after the severe recession of 1980–1982 with (up to now) low inflation, which started in December 1982, points in the same direction. In fact, the performance of the U.S. economy in recent years has surpassed that of Western Europe, thus contradicting the view held by proponents of industrial policy that the United States is falling behind other industrial countries.

The strong rebound of the automobile industry, which was hit very hard by imports and the recession, is another striking example of private enterprise strongly adjusting to changing conditions. True, the industry was assisted (at high cost to the U.S. consumer) by "voluntary" restrictions imposed on Japanese exporters. But this does not change the fact that the industry displayed entrepreneurial talent by cutting labor costs, installing labor-saving machinery, tightening work schedules, improving quality, and wresting wage and work rule concessions from the unions. The industry is still suffering from an excessively high wage level; automobile wages (like wages in the steel industry) are far above the average wage in U.S. manufacturing industries. But given this handicap, the industry has done a credible job of adjusting to foreign competition and recession.[4]

The conclusion I draw from all of this is that there is nothing senile about U.S industry, there is no lack of entrepreneurial talent, and industry can and does adjust to changing conditions. It is naive to assume that the government—or more precisely some existing government agencies or some new ad hoc ones, such as a U.S. "development bank"—could do a better job than private enterprise of identifying and developing new "growth industries" or induce or coax existing industries or firms to adjust more quickly and efficiently to changing conditions. The policy would be an administrative nightmare, and the predictable results would be much wasted effort and the government's finding itself holding a number of white elephants.

There is a danger that the adoption of industrial policy measures by some states may subvert or erode the constitutional guarantee of free trade within the United States. The Constitution says: "No Taxes or Duty shall be laid on articles exported from any state" (Article I, section 9, clause 5).

Protectionists and other representatives of special interests know that it is possible to achieve their aims by some sort of subsidy, if for one reason or another it cannot be done by import duties or export bounties. Many states or municipalities have granted special tax incentives to individual firms to set up shop there. The danger is that under the banner of industrial policy such interventionist-protectionist policies will be pursued systematically on a large scale. Many state governors and legislatures are moving in that direction. In Rhode Island a very ambitious scheme called the Greenhouse Compact was actually voted by the legislature and put to a popular vote. It provides for elaborate procedures to pick "promising" growth areas to be subsidized in various ways. The accompanying report runs to over a thousand pages. Similar plans are being actively considered in many other states. Fortunately the Rhode Island proposal was rejected decisively at the polls because the voters resented the tax increase that it would have entailed. But there is still a danger that the proponents of industrial policy will continue their drive and find more attractive packaging for their schemes.[5]

A striking example of the danger of industrial policy is provided by France. The Socialist government of François Mitterrand, which came to power in 1981, has engaged in industrial policy in a grand manner, although it does not call it industrial policy but simply Socialism—what it really is. A large number of leading industrial corporations were nationalized because they were regarded as promising candidates to be turned into showpieces of rapid industrial development. It did not turn out that way. Despite huge infusions of additional capital at the taxpayers' expense, most of the nationalized enterprises have suffered large losses and have become a heavy burden on the government budget, contributing mightily to the ongoing inflation and crowding out private investment.

The vacuousness of the concept is revealed by the fact that, in reply to criticism, advocates of industrial policy now say that the United States and all other industrial countries have their industrial policy anyway. Robert B. Reich, one of the leading proponents of industrial policy, puts it this way: "A nation's industrial policy is the sum of its microeconomic policies—like tax rules, research and development grants, credit subsidies, and import restrictions—as they affect the pace and direction of industrial change. Every advanced nation has an industrial policy."[6]

It thus seems that industrial policy can be defined as an effort to improve and streamline micropolicies. In the abstract this sounds reasonable. But the proposed concrete measures would subject the economy to more and more controls. The proponents of industrial policy have failed to realize that the most effective way to improve the performance of the economy is to promote competition and to eliminate micromeasures that stifle it. Free trade and deregulation of industry should be high on the list. As I have mentioned, the deregulation of the airline and trucking industries in the United States has been a great success.

Under free trade few monopolies would survive. We have seen that the superior performance of the U.S. economy compared with Europe's economy is in large part due to the fact that the United States enjoys the tremendous advantage of a large internal free trade area and that private enterprise prevails in transportation, communications, and electric power.[7]

Notes

1. "Why Europe Has Failed," *The Economist* (London), November 24, 1984, p. 13.

2. See John R. Meyer and Robert A. Leone, "The New England States and Their Economic Future: Some Implications of a Changing Industrial Environment," *Papers and Proceedings of the American Economic Association*, vol. 68 (May 1978), pp. 110–15; and Lynn E. Browne and John S. Hekman, "New England's Economy in the 1980s," *New England Economic Review* (Federal Reserve Bank of Boston) (January/February 1981).

3. "California's Economy: A Survey," *The Economist* (London), May 19, 1984.

4. Needless to say, this should not be interpreted as a justification of protection. On the contrary, as pointed out in chapter 9, the existing restrictions of imports by quotas on Japanese exporters is the worst possible arrangement, much worse than an import tariff would be.

5. For further details see Walter Olson, "Industrial Policy from the Grass Roots?" *Wall Street Journal*, June 12, 1984.

6. Robert B. Reich, "An Industrial Policy of the Right," *The Public Interest*, no. 73 (Fall 1983).

7. An excellent comprehensive discussion of industrial policy can be found in the *1984 Report of the Council of Economic Advisers*. It includes a good analysis of the vaunted industrial policies in Japan and some European countries. Since this was written another excellent study, by Robert Z. Lawrence, *Can America Compete?* (Washington, D.C.: Brookings Institution, 1984), has appeared. Lawrence examines the performance of the U.S. economy "in historical and global perspective," reaching roughly the same conclusion as the CEA report and this paper: that, contrary to what proponents of an industrial policy say, "there has been no tendency of a deindustrialization" of the U.S. economy resulting from competition from other countries that are supposedly doing much better than the United States.

A NOTE ON THE BOOK

This book was edited by
Gertrude Kaplan and Donna Spitler.
Pat Taylor designed the cover,
and Hördur Karlsson drew the figure.
The text was set in Palatino, a typeface
designed by Hermann Zapf.
Hendricks-Miller Typographic Company,
of Washington, D.C., set the type, and
Thomson-Shore, Inc., of Dexter, Michigan,
printed and bound the book,
using permanent, acid-free paper made by the
S.D. Warren Company.

SELECTED AEI PUBLICATIONS

Essays in Contemporary Economic Problems, 1985: The Economy in Deficit, Phillip Cagan, ed. (1985, 336 pp., cloth $20.95, paper $9.95)

Essays in Contemporary Economic Problems: Disinflation, William Fellner, project director (1983, 324 pp., cloth $19.95, paper $10.95)

Trade in Services: A Case for Open Markets, Jonathan David Aronson and Peter F. Cowhey (1984, 46 pp., $3.95)

High-Technology Policies: A Five-Nation Comparison, Richard R. Nelson (1984, 94 pp., cloth $13.95, paper $4.95)

Controlling the Cost of Social Security, Colin D. Campbell, ed. (1984, 269 pp., $26.00)

Maintaining the Safety Net: Income Redistribution Programs in the Reagan Administration, John C. Weicher, ed. (1984, 204 pp., cloth $17.95, paper $9.95)

The R&D Tax Credit: Issues in Tax Policy and Industrial Innovation, Kenneth M. Brown, ed. (1984, 47 pp., $4.95)

• *Mail orders for publications to:* AMERICAN ENTERPRISE INSTITUTE, 1150 Seventeenth Street, N.W., Washington, D.C. 20036 • *For postage and handling, add 10 percent of total; minimum charge $2, maximum $10 (no charge on prepaid orders)* • *For information on orders, or to expedite service, call toll free 800-424-2873 (in Washington, D.C., 202-862-5869)* • *Prices subject to change without notice.* • *Payable in U.S. currency through U.S. banks only*

AEI ASSOCIATES PROGRAM

The American Enterprise Institute invites your participation in the competition of ideas through its AEI Associates Program. This program has two objectives: (1) to extend public familiarity with contemporary issues; and (2) to increase research on these issues and disseminate the results to policy makers, the academic community, journalists, and others who help shape public policies. The areas studied by AEI include Economic Policy, Education Policy, Energy Policy, Fiscal Policy, Government Regulation, Health Policy, International Programs, Legal Policy, National Defense Studies, Political and Social Processes, and Religion, Philosophy, and Public Policy. For the $49 annual fee, Associates receive

- a subscription to *Memorandum*, the newsletter on all AEI activities
- the AEI publications catalog and all supplements
- a 30 percent discount on all AEI books
- a 40 percent discount for certain seminars on key issues
- subscriptions to any two of the following publications: *Public Opinion*, a bimonthly magazine exploring trends and implications of public opinion on social and public policy questions; *Regulation*, a bimonthly journal examining all aspects of government regulation of society; and *AEI Economist*, a monthly newsletter analyzing current economic issues and evaluating future trends (or for all three publications, send an additional $12).

Call 202/862-6446 or write: AMERICAN ENTERPRISE INSTITUTE
1150 Seventeenth Street, N.W., Suite 301, Washington, D.C. 20036